French–Beaded Flowers

Dalene Kelly

David & Charles

A DAVID & CHARLES BOOK

First published in the UK in 2004
First published in the USA as More French Beaded Flowers by Krause publications,
an F&W Publications company, in 2004

A catalogue record for this book is available from the British Library.

ISBN 0 7153 1882 9

Printed in the USA by CJ Krehbiel
for David & Charles
Brunel House   Newton Abbot   Devon

Visit our website at www.davidandcharles.co.uk

David & Charles books are available from all good bookshops; alternatively you can contact our Orderline on (0)1626 334555 or write to us at FREEPOST EX2110, David & Charles Direct, Newton Abbot, TQ12 4ZZ (no stamp required UK mainland).

Edited by Maria L. Turner
Designed by Marilyn McGrane

Dedication

For me, the dedication is the most difficult part of completing a book. How can a person possibly thank all the people who enriched her life? How can one decide who was the most influential in bringing about her present circumstances?

So, to name just a few, I dedicate this book:

- To my mother, Virgene McGroarty, who allowed me the freedom to choose my own path.
- To my mother-in-law, Sally Kelly, who taught me to bead flowers.
- To my daddy, James McGroarty, who was kind beyond description, as even his last moments were spent worrying about those he left behind.
- To my husband, Van Kelly, who is the love of my life.

Acknowledgments

I would like to thank all the wonderful people at Krause Publications for making this book "happen." In particular, many thanks to:

- Graphic artist Marilyn McGrane, who made my goofy drawings look professional and who made the cover and interior pages a thing of beauty.
- Photographer Robert Best, who not only "knows his stuff," but also knows when not to laugh out loud.
- The members of the editorial staff who held my hand and dried my tears when I saw what the shipping company had done to my flowers.

Table of Contents

Introduction 6
Getting Started 7
  • Materials, Tools, and Supplies 8
  • General Instructions 12

Flower Patterns 21
  • Lollipop Plant 22
  • Bromeliad (Pink Flame) 25
  • Spider Mum 28
  • Small Sunflower 30
  • Hummingbird 34
  • Trumpet Vine 38
  • Bougainvillea 42
  • Peony 44
  • Eucalyptus Stems 47
  • Dendrobium Orchid 48
  • Spiderwort 50
  • Plumeria 52
  • Cattleya Orchid 55
  • Golden Grain 58
  • Ghost Orchid 61
  • Carnation 64
  • Lilac 67
  • Floribunda Rose 70
  • Columbine 73
  • Freesia 76
  • Passion Flower and Fruit 79
  • Lily of the Valley 82
  • Bee 84
  • Dragonfly 86
  • Lady Slipper Orchid 88
  • Miniatures 91
  • Swallowtail Butterfly 94
  • Tulip Poplar 97
  • Geranium 100
  • Bird of Paradise 103
  • Mexican Thistle 106
  • Texas Bluebonnet 108
  • Bonsai Tree 111
  • Large Sunflower 114
  • Christmas Cactus 117
  • Poinsettia with Pinecone
      and Branch 120
  • Pickle Ornament 124

Resources 126
About the Author 127

Introduction

"French beading" is a beautiful and timeless art. It allows every individual the opportunity to create pieces that are distinctly her own.

As noted in my first book, *French-Beaded Flowers: New Millennium Collection* (Krause Publications, 2001), the art of French beading most likely began with French and other European peasants who collected discarded glass beads and used them to create arrangements and flowered memorial wreaths. Because of the work and skill involved in creating these beautiful "works of art," beaded flowers have always been collectible and timeless treasures. Many antique flowers can be found in museums, as well as in numerous private collections, all over the world. According to the French Beading Artists Guild of Idaho Falls, Idaho, a few notable people who owned and treasured examples of this fine art were: Marie Antoinette, Madam Pompadour, Napoleon's Josephine, Princess Grace, Princess Caroline, Patricia Nixon, and William Randolph Hearst.

Today, you will often see French beading grouped with other beading techniques, but it is really much more like sculpting than sewing. The beads are strung onto wire, and that wire is bent and twisted to form the flower pieces that are then assembled into beautiful displays.

Because every French-bead artist has her own style and taste, I do not presume to choose your bead colors or wire types. Items listed in the project patterns are meant only as suggestions. Once you have mastered the fundamentals, feel free to experiment with different wires and beads of varying shapes, types, colors, and sizes. Add or subtract a few rows, here or there, to achieve a different look. Some of the items in this book are shown in miniature arrangements and could easily be adapted to full-size arrangements, if desired. Simply grab some ideas and "run with them." Most importantly, have fun and feel free to express your own style!

Happy beading,
Dalene Kelly

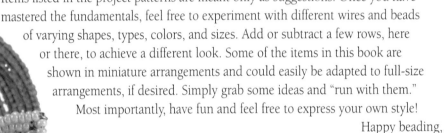

Note Regarding the use of beaded flowers in memorial wreaths: I am delighted to say that this tradition has been carried forward. After the September 11, 2001, terrorist attacks on the United States, a group of nearly 100 contributors from six countries (including the U.S.) made more than 800 beaded flowers and pieces of beaded greenery. These items were assembled into three separate wreaths. At the date of this printing, one wreath has already been delivered to the Pentagon. Another is in the National Liberty Museum in Philadelphia and the third is awaiting a home in New York. The entire project was completed on a volunteer basis.

Before you begin in the art of French beading, you will want to familiarize yourself with some of the basic tools and techniques. This section covers the basics—the fundamentals a beginner will need to get started. Of course, if you aren't a novice, feel free to skip ahead to the patterns and just use this section as a reference, when and if needed.

Getting Started

Materials, Tools, and Supplies

BEADS

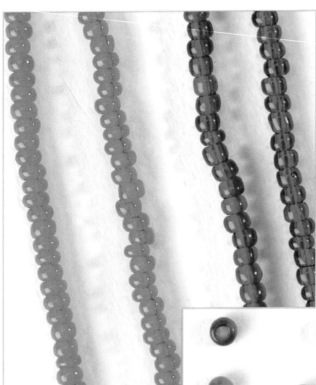

Above: Seed beads that come on strands, which are sold as hanks, are the easiest to use when creating French-beaded flowers.

Right: Loose seed beads can be used either as they are, or with the help of a bead spinner.

Finish

For best results, begin by choosing beads that appear uniform in size and shape. They can be found in transparent, opaque (shiny, silk, or matte), pearl (painted), and lined finishes.

Although transparent, opaque, and pearl finishes can be used interchangeably, lined beads may present some special challenges. The lining materials in these beads can deteriorate over a period of time. Sunshine, cleaning products, and sometimes even the act of stringing the beads can ruin the color. Having said that, some colors, especially pinks and purples, are only available in lined beads. Just use and clean them with tender-loving care.

Shape

Round seed beads are the beads of choice. However, particularly on very large flowers, cut seed beads can produce a very elegant effect.

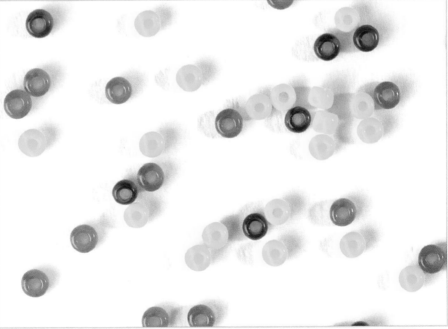

Size

To reproduce the flowers in this book, choose either size 10/0 or size 11/0 seed beads. Size 10/0 beads are slightly larger and will look a little less delicate than the size 11/0 beads. However, you can use any size desired to achieve many different styles. The chart shown here gives you an idea of the sizes of seed beads available.

Seed Bead Sizes	
7/0	4mm
8/0	3.1mm
9/0	2.7mm
10/0	**2.3mm**
11/0	**2.1mm**
12/0	1.9mm
13/0	1.7mm
14/0	1.6mm

Quantities

All of the quantities given in the patterns are estimates. I recommend buying extra, since it is better to have a few more than is needed than not enough. Here is a rough estimate of quantities:
- 16 to 17 beads per inch
- 18" per strand
- 12 strands per hank
- 20 to 24 hanks per kilo (2.2 pounds)

Seed beads are available either loose or strung. For ease and speed, you will probably be much happier finding a supplier that carries strung beads (mostly from the Czech Republic). If you can't find them locally, hanks are available on the Internet (see Resources, page 126). Loose beads can also be used easily if you invest a little more money and purchase a bead spinner (or stringer).

Several examples of the colors and types of wire used in French beading.

WIRE

Color

Try to match your wire to your beads as closely as possible. A wide range of colors, as well as gold and silver, can be found in the jewelry and bead departments of your local craft store.

Finish

Wire is metal, and metal rusts. Therefore, my first choice is always a painted or electroplated wire. For a more economical source of green, black, and white, check out the paddle wire in floral and bridal departments. I really like 30-gauge floral paddle wire for all of my assembly. It's inexpensive, and it won't show once the flower is taped.

Wire Gauges		
N/A	.125" (1/8")	3.2mm
16	.063"	1.6mm
18	.048"	1.2mm
20	.035"	.88mm
22	.029"	.73mm
24	.023"	.58mm
26	.018"	.46mm
28	.016"	.41mm
30	.014"	.36mm
32	.013"	.33mm
34	.012"	.30mm

Sizes

You will probably use a 26- to 28-gauge painted wire or 24- to 26-gauge electroplated wire for most flower parts. If you have trouble handling the wire, experiment with different sizes and materials. The accompanying chart provides a listing of wire sizes by gauge, inches, and millimeters to help you understand what sizes are available. The ultimate decision on the best wire choice is dependent on your personal preferences.

When making greenery, the most economical wire is floral paddle wire.
Use 30-gauge wire for assembly and lacing.
Stem wire is available in precut painted lengths in the floral department. Here are some suggested sizes:
• Small flowers, 18-gauge
  • Medium to large flowers, 14- to 16-gauge
  • Large or unbalanced flowers (i.e. orchid plants), 1/8" round rod stock, threaded rod stock or cut-up coat hangers

TOOLS AND SUPPLIES

Bead spinner: Used to spin many beads directly onto a thread, which is an ideal timesaving device for stringing loose beads. (optional)

Darning needle: Used for lacing large leaves and petals. (optional)

Divided or flat lunch tray: Used to keep loose beads in your work area from falling on the floor. Be sure to lay or glue felt inside the sections. (optional)

Flat, long nose pliers: Used for stretching and straightening bent wire.

Floral tape: Used to wrap exposed wire, especially stems. Available in most floral departments, the regular wax-coated paper tape works best.

Hem gauge or ruler: Used to measure and ensure petals are uniform. The hem gauge is preferred because it can be set to the size needed.

Hemostats or locking pliers: Used for twisting wires. They are available in craft, medical, hardware, or sporting goods stores.

Needle nose pliers: Used for bending and manipulating wire. Choose ones with cutters and you can also use them for cutting heavy stem wires so your regular wire cutters can last longer.

Scissors: Used for cutting. Choose a pair that is small, sharp, and comfortable-to-use.

Wire cutters: Used to cut wire. Choose comfortable-to-use, sharp, hobby or jewelry front-cutters. Side-cutters are more difficult to handle.

Flat nose pliers.

Floral tape.

Hem gauge.

Hemostats.

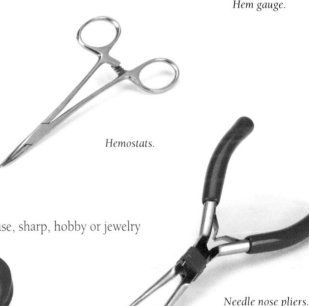

Wire cutters.

Needle nose pliers.

Scissors.

General Instructions

UNDERSTANDING FLOWER PARTS

When creating French-beaded flowers, it's necessary to familiarize yourself with the basic parts of a flower. Figure 1 diagrams the common names for the parts of the flower, giving you a quick reference. If a flower doesn't include one of these parts, don't panic. This is an art, not a science.

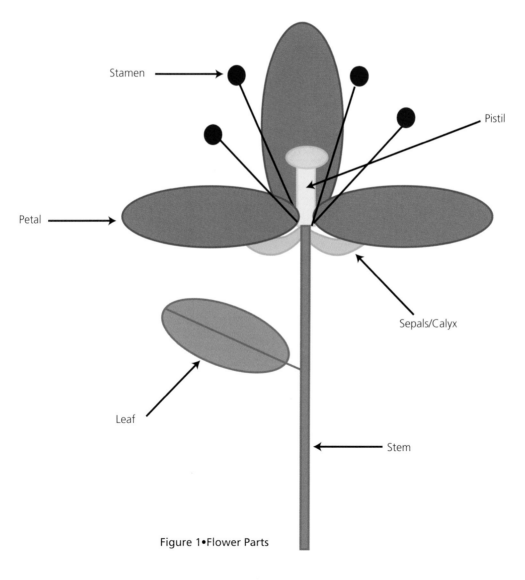

Stamen

Pistil

Petal

Sepals/Calyx

Leaf

Stem

Figure 1•Flower Parts

BASIC METHOD

Creating a Beaded Piece

1•Begin by transferring your beads onto the spool of wire. If using beads on hanks, hold the string taut and slide the wire through several inches at a time. If using loose beads, "spear" them onto the wire one at a time, or use a bead spinner. (This little gadget can string beads at an amazing rate.) Put enough beads on the wire to complete the entire petal or leaf. Err on the side of excess.

2•Determine (from the pattern) the size of your "basic" beaded row. Count (or measure) the required number of seed beads and slide them toward the wire tip, leaving several inches of bare basic wire. Hold the beads in place by pinching the wire below them.

3•Wrap the wire end loosely around your hand, forming the "basic loop." Bring the wire end up under the beads and twist several times (Figure 2). If you have trouble keeping your basic row on the wire, try bending the tip of the wire into a tight loop before beginning. You will now be wrapping beads up one side and down the other of the first basic row.

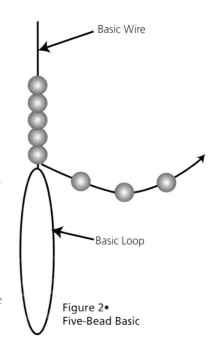

Basic Wire

Basic Loop

**Figure 2•
Five-Bead Basic**

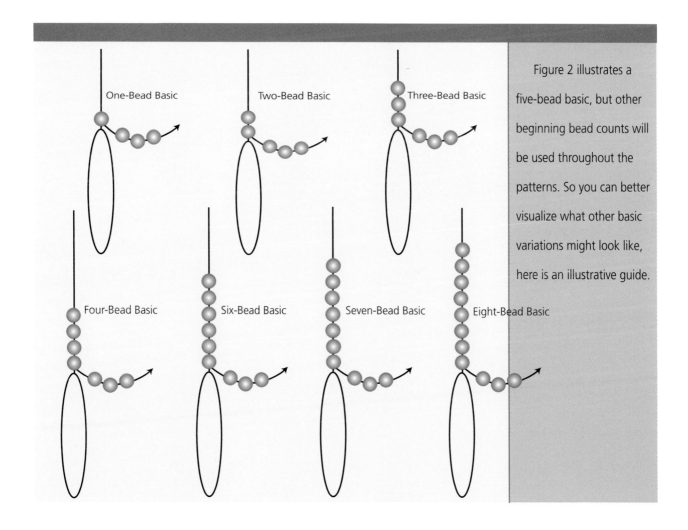

One-Bead Basic

Two-Bead Basic

Three-Bead Basic

Four-Bead Basic

Six-Bead Basic

Seven-Bead Basic

Eight-Bead Basic

Figure 2 illustrates a five-bead basic, but other beginning bead counts will be used throughout the patterns. So you can better visualize what other basic variations might look like, here is an illustrative guide.

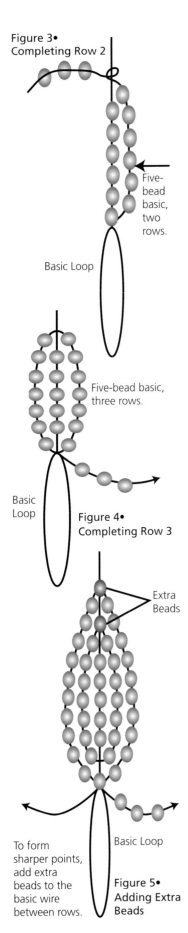

Figure 3•
Completing Row 2

Five-bead basic, two rows.

Basic Loop

Five-bead basic, three rows.

Basic Loop

Figure 4•
Completing Row 3

Extra Beads

To form sharper points, add extra beads to the basic wire between rows.

Basic Loop

Figure 5•
Adding Extra Beads

4•Keeping your basic wire straight at all times, push some beads forward from the spool, and bring the wire to the top of the basic row. Cross over and then under the basic wire and pull the wire tight (Figure 3).

5•Repeat step 4 down the other side of the basic row. Rows are counted straight across the center, so you have now completed three rows (Figure 4).

6•Proceed in the same manner as in steps 4 and 5, until you have the desired number of rows.

To form a rounded petal: Keep the wire very close and straight across the top of the previous row when crossing the basic wire.

To form a pointed petal: Cross the basic wire at a 45° angle, leaving a very slight space before your over-and-under twist as in step 4 of the Basic Method.

To form an exaggerated point: Add an extra bead to the top of your basic wire, between the rows (Figure 5). This is not mentioned in most patterns, but it can be used to accomplish the desired effect. Long, narrow, pointed leaves and petals are especially enhanced by the use of extra beads.

Wire-Cutting Options

Three wires (stiff): Cut the basic loop open at the bottom, pull out some spool wire, and cut the spool wire to the same length as the basic loop wires and twist (Figure 6).

Two wires (medium): Cut the spool wire ½" from the bottom of the piece, cut open the bottom of the basic loop, and twist (Figure 7).

One wire (light): Cut both the spool wire and one side of the basic loop ½" from the piece and twist (Figure 8).

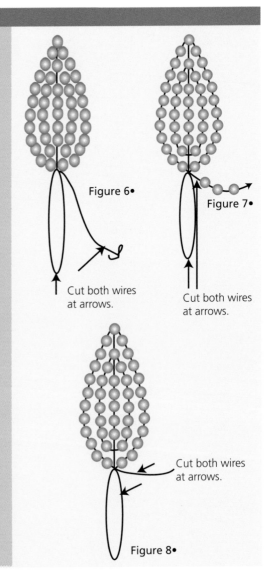

Figure 6•

Cut both wires at arrows.

Figure 7•

Cut both wires at arrows.

Cut both wires at arrows.

Figure 8•

7 • To end the petal/leaf, check the pattern to determine the number of wires you should have remaining. Use one of the options detailed in the sidebar to cut the wire from the spool. The bulkiness of the wires during construction and the support needed for each petal will determine how you should cut the piece from the spool. The more wires you leave, the stiffer it will be.

8 • Cut the top section of the basic wire to a ¼" length and fold it down tightly against the back of the piece (Figure 9).

9 • Twist the bottom wires by grabbing the wire ends with the locking hemostats in one hand and holding the flower part in the other hand. Put the middle finger of the hemostat hand through one of the handle loops, pull tight, and rotate your wrist (Figure 10). The result is a smooth, even stem that will not fall apart later. Caution: Twist only until smooth and even; if you get carried away, you'll lose your stem!

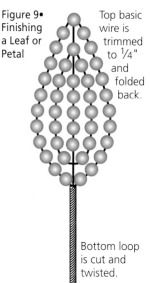

Figure 9•
Finishing a Leaf or Petal

Top basic wire is trimmed to ¼" and folded back.

Bottom loop is cut and twisted.

Hold tightly.

Put one finger through a handle loop and rotate your wrist.

Figure 10•
Using Hemostats

10 • On long or wide pieces, it is necessary to lace the rows together in order to get a smooth and neat appearance. Refer to the Lacing Techniques (Figure 11) that follow for assistance with this step. There are two options when it comes to lacing, as detailed below.

Option 1

1 • Thread a piece of 30-gauge (or finer) wire through a darning needle and twist the needle to secure the wire.

2 • Beginning in the center of the back of the piece, use an over-and-under motion to weave the wire to the outside edge. Then turn (running stitch) and use the same stitch to weave back across to the far edge. Turn and weave back to the center.

3 • Pull the ends together, twist, and cut (Figure 11, left).

Option 2

1 • Thread a piece of 30-gauge (or finer) wire through a darning needle and twist the needle to secure the wire.

2 • Beginning at the edge of the back of the piece, twist the loose end of the wire around the outside row of beads and use a backstitch to work across to the far edge.

3 • Twist the end around the last row again to secure and trim (Figure 11, right).

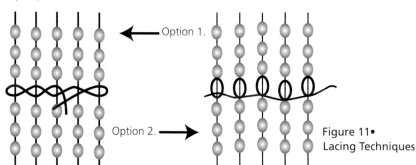

Option 1.

Option 2.

Figure 11•
Lacing Techniques

11 • To finish the piece, tape the exposed wire with floral tape. You may also choose to bead, floss, or otherwise cover the stems. However, be sure to tape them first. The tape waterproofs the wire and provides a good non-skid base for anything you may choose to add later.

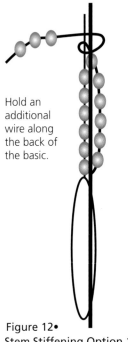

Hold an additional wire along the back of the basic.

Figure 12•
Stem Stiffening Option 1

Stem Stiffening

Depending on the type of leaves you are working with, you will need to choose one of the following two options to stiffen the stem sufficiently to support your leaves.

Option 1 (for long, slender leaves)

For long, slender leaves that are meant to stand up straight, incorporate an additional stem wire into the construction.

1• After you measure your basic row of beads, hold the extra, light-gauge stem wire against the back of the beads.

2• On each round, wrap the bead wire around both the extra and the basic wires.

3• When the leaf is finished, trim and twist the extra wire right along with the basic wire (Figure 12).

Option 2 (for large, round leaves)

For large, round leaves that just need support at the base, add only enough wire to thicken the short, twisted stem.

1• After the leaf is completed, but before you twist the stem wire, cut a piece of wire that is twice as long as the distance from the bottom of the basic wire to the top of the lower, wrapped area.

2• Fold the cut piece of wire in half.

3• From the right side of the leaf, insert one end of the folded wire at the bottom between rows 1 and 2.

4• Insert the other end of the folded wire at the bottom between rows 1 and 3.

5• Lightly twist the entire length of the cut wire.

6• Combine the twisted wire with the stem wires and twist again (Figure 13).

Figure 13•
Stem Stiffening Option 2

Taping

Floral tape is usually found in ½" widths. Use as is, or for ease in handling when working on small pieces, remove a length of tape, cut it in half lengthwise, and use the ¼" tape for taping small stems and leaves.

1• Lightly stretch the tape to activate the wax.

2• Hold the tip against the bloom end of the wire and twirl the wire between your fingers as you move the tape downward. This will create a tight, smooth spiral.

3• Once the entire area is covered, tear off the tape.

4• Pinch, smooth, and rub the stem so that the tape edges fuse together (Figure 14).

Flossing Stems

This is done just like, but over the top of, your tape. The most elegant type of floss to use is untwisted silk. Because untwisted silk is very expensive and extremely difficult to find, feel free to experiment with a range of different materials, including rayon floss and colored raffia.

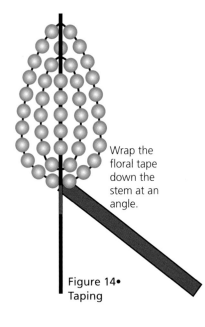

Wrap the floral tape down the stem at an angle.

Figure 14•
Taping

Beading Stems

This treatment is most impressive on large flowers and branches.

For small stems and branches:

1· Tape wires first and string at least 5 feet of beads onto spooled wire.

2· Allowing about 2" of bare wire to trail down the stem, hold the bare end of the wire tight against the bottom of the bud and wrap tightly twice around the stem.

3· Slide the beads forward on the wire and hold them tightly in place while wrapping them around and down the stem (just as with taping). I keep my other thumbnail tight against the previously wound row. Then, as I wrap the next time around, the new row actually pushes my thumbnail down the stem.

4· When you get to a leaf, pull the leaf downward and bead tight into the crevice.

5· Pull the leaf back up and bead around until you meet it again.

6· Let the beads slide back and wrap the bare wire once around the base of the leaf.

7· Push the beads back up the wire and continue to wrap the beads down to the point where the stems (branches) meet.

8· End here by wrapping the bare wire several times around the stem, as close to the beads as possible.

9· Spiral the bare wire down a few inches before cutting.

10· Repeat the entire process for the rest of the small stems and branches.

For the main stem:

1· After wiring the branches together, wrap the stem in the same manner as step 1 of the smaller stems and branches. If you have enough room, start your bead wrapping by putting the first row of beads between the petals and the sepals.

2· Wrap the bare wire around each sepal, just as you did the leaf on the bud stem, and continue as in step 3 of the small stem and branches instructions.

3· Do not cut the wire when you reach the joints. Instead, wrap the bare wire once around each joint and continue downward.

4· Stop at least 1" to 3" from the bottom and end as in steps 8 and 9 of the previous instructions.

5· Cut the wire and cover all exposed ends with floral tape.

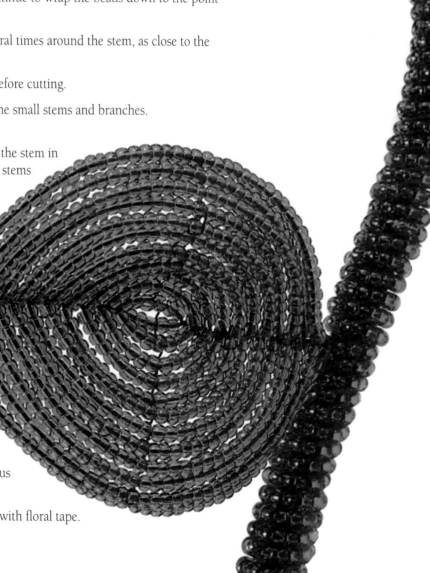

OTHER COMMONLY USED TECHNIQUES

Continuous Loops

1•Without a basic wire, form a loop of beads in the desired length, cross the wires, and give one full twist (Figure 15, left).

2•Beginning at the base of the loop just completed, repeat the process for the desired number of loops (Figure 15, right).

Figure 15•
Single
and Single
Continuous
Loops

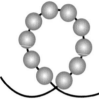

Use at least one full twist at the bottom of each loop. (Always twist all of the loops in the same direction.)

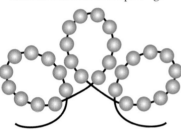

Continuous Double Loops

1•Use the same technique as the continuous loops (step 1) to form the first loop.

2•Wrap beads around the outside of the first loop, creating a second loop (Figure 16, left).

3•Twist and move on to the next loop, repeating the process for the desired number of loops (Figure 16, right).

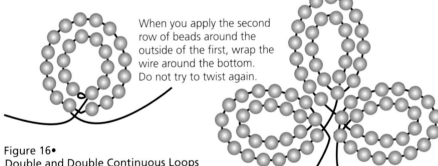

When you apply the second row of beads around the outside of the first, wrap the wire around the bottom. Do not try to twist again.

Figure 16•
Double and Double Continuous Loops

Continuous Crossover Loops

1•Beginning with the continuous loop technique (step 1), make the loop, twist to secure, and then bead up the front of the loop and down the back.

2•Twist and move on to the next loop. This makes a four-row crossover loop.

3•For the three-row crossover, bead up the front and leave bare wire down the back.

4•Twist and move on to the next loop (Figure 17).

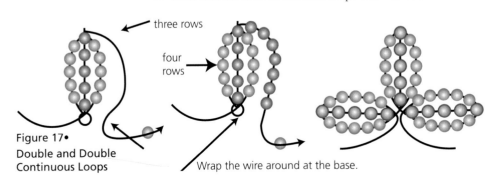

three rows

four rows

Figure 17•
Double and Double
Continuous Loops

Wrap the wire around at the base.

Continuous Loop-Backs

1•Make your first and second continuous loops (steps 1 and 2).

2•Twist the wire back around the base of the first loop, go to the other side, and make loop 3.

3•Continue in this manner for the desired number of loops (Figure 18).

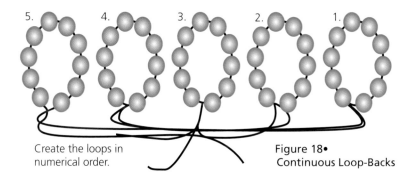

Create the loops in
numerical order.

Figure 18•
Continuous Loop-Backs

Beehive (Cup)

This technique is accomplished by bending the basic wire, the basic loop, or both, backwards, at a set angle, while continuing to add rows. A slight bend of both wires will form a type of raised-button shape, similar to the center of a daisy. A sharp bend of one wire will create a tapered cup (snapdragon petal). A sharp bend of both basics will create a thimble shape (coneflower center). See Figure 19 for side views.

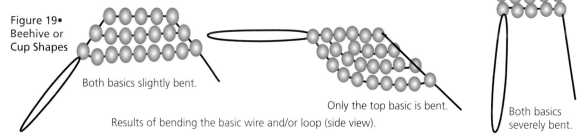

Figure 19•
Beehive or
Cup Shapes

Both basics slightly bent.

Only the top basic is bent.

Results of bending the basic wire and/or loop (side view).

Both basics
severely bent.

Weaving or Basket Bottom

This technique looks just as it sounds. However, you don't actually weave over and under the wires. Instead, every time you come to one of the spread wires (spokes), you wrap the wire around it, as if it were the basic wire.

1•Cut a determined number of wires.

2•Hold wires together in a bundle and wrap the bare end of the beaded wire twice, tightly around the centers.

3•Spread the wires open, like the spokes of a wheel, and bead around the center. (Some patterns will tell you how many beads to put between the spokes; others will not.) These are counted as rounds, instead of rows (Figure 20).

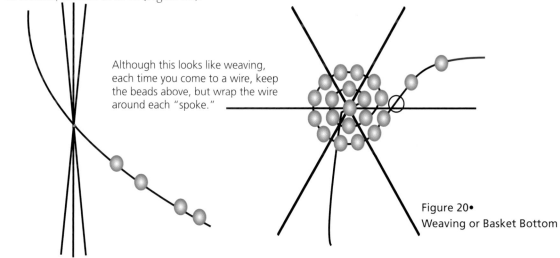

Although this looks like weaving,
each time you come to a wire, keep
the beads above, but wrap the wire
around each "spoke."

Figure 20•
Weaving or Basket Bottom

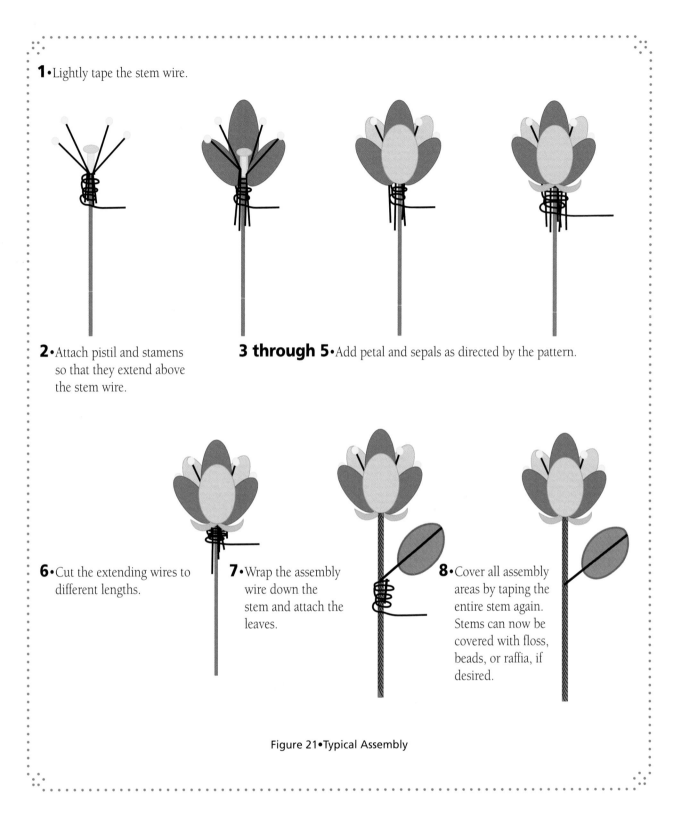

1•Lightly tape the stem wire.

2•Attach pistil and stamens so that they extend above the stem wire.

3 through 5•Add petal and sepals as directed by the pattern.

6•Cut the extending wires to different lengths.

7•Wrap the assembly wire down the stem and attach the leaves.

8•Cover all assembly areas by taping the entire stem again. Stems can now be covered with floss, beads, or raffia, if desired.

Figure 21•Typical Assembly

Shading

In this book, the Tulip Poplar, the Swallowtail Butterfly, and one of the Small Sunflowers employ the techniques required to shade petals.

This is done by cutting a piece of wire and feeding the beads onto the long end of the wire, as needed. Achieving desired results often requires trial and error.

Flower Patterns

The patterns contained within this section offer something for everyone interested in French beading—regardless of your skill level. As a beginner, the patterns will familiarize you with a wide range of techniques, shapes, and styles. (Be sure to note the illustrations represent the techniques used and do not show actual bead counts.) The seasoned beader should find the patterns beneficial as a new source of inspiration.

Lollipop Plant

Materials

- 1 hank bright yellow 11/0 seed beads
- 1 hank dark green 11/0 seed beads
- 4 strands white 11/0 seed beads
- 26-gauge gold beading wire
- 26-gauge green beading or paddle wire
- 30-gauge assembly wire
- 2 18"-long 16-gauge stem wires
- ½" green floral tape
- ½" yellow floral tape*
  *Yellow floral tape is suggested, but if you are not able to find yellow tape, use yellow floss in the finishing process.

Bracts (pointed top, round bottom)

Make 8 (yellow): three-bead basic, three rows.
1•Do not cut the top basic wires.
2•Reduce each to one wire and twist.

Make 8 (yellow): three-bead basic, five rows.
Reduce each to one wire and twist.

Make 8 (yellow): three-bead basic, seven rows.
Reduce each to one wire and twist.

Make 8 (yellow): three-bead basic, nine rows.
Reduce each to one wire and twist.

Make 8 (yellow): three-bead basic, 11 rows.
Reduce each to one wire and twist.

Make 4 (yellow): three-bead basic, 13 rows.

Buds (crossover loops)

Make 8 (white) as follows:
1•Leave 2" of bare wire.
2•Using 2" of beads for the first loop, make one four-row crossover loop.
3•End with 2" of bare wire, cut, and twist.
4•Flatten the bud and put a slight "sideways" bend in the buds.

Flowers (continuous loops)

Make 4 (white) as follows:
1•Leave 2" of bare wire.
2•Using 2" of beads for the first loop, make one two-row continuous loop.
3•Make one 1½" loop of beads.
4•End with 2" of bare wire, cut, and twist.
5•Tape with yellow floral tape.

Leaves (pointed top, pointed bottom)

Make 2 (green): ¾" basic, 11 rows.
1•Leave three wires, twist, and lace.
2•Tape ½" of the stem, closest to the beads.

Make 2 (green): 1" basic, 11 rows.
1•Leave three wires, twist, and lace.
2•Tape ½" of the stem, closest to the beads.

Make 2 (green): 1¼" basic, 17 rows.
1•Leave three wires, twist, and lace.
2•Tape ½" of the stem, closest to the beads.

Make 2 (green): 1¼" basic, 19 rows.
1•Leave three wires, twist, and lace.
2•Tape ½" of the stem, closest to the beads.

On a cold, snowy day, I wandered into my local garden center for inspiration. There, I found a recent shipment of tropical flowers to immortalize. The lollipop plant was one of my first choices. Simple, white flowers seem to explode from nearly fluorescent yellow torches. If the look is too haphazard for your tastes, leave out the white flowers.

lollipop plant

Notice the bend of the bracts, as well as the careful positioning of the flowers.

ASSEMBLY

1· Lightly tape both stem wires. Use yellow tape on the top 4".

2· On the four smallest bracts, bend the top basic wires backwards 90 degrees.

3· Place smallest bracts face down with their tips together, twist the top wires, and cut to ¼".

4· Bend these bracts upward, enclosing the twisted wires inside. Use assembly wire to attach to the yellow end of a stem wire.

5· Plan the position of your flowers. Each "lollipop" will have four sides. The flowers appear at the same level, as do the buds. The buds are also above the flowers. Therefore, choose four bracts of the same size and position four buds (flowers) along the backside of each. Make sure that the flower extends far enough that it can be bent down over the front of the bract. Twist the wires together.

6· Using the next largest bracts, secure four directly below the tip bracts. The tips of these should be centered and two-thirds of the bract down from the previous row.

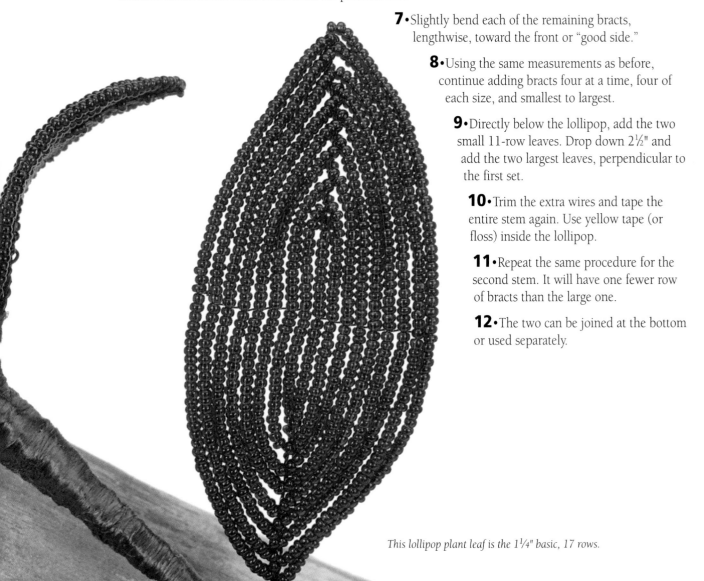

7· Slightly bend each of the remaining bracts, lengthwise, toward the front or "good side."

8· Using the same measurements as before, continue adding bracts four at a time, four of each size, and smallest to largest.

9· Directly below the lollipop, add the two small 11-row leaves. Drop down 2½" and add the two largest leaves, perpendicular to the first set.

10· Trim the extra wires and tape the entire stem again. Use yellow tape (or floss) inside the lollipop.

11· Repeat the same procedure for the second stem. It will have one fewer row of bracts than the large one.

12· The two can be joined at the bottom or used separately.

This lollipop plant leaf is the 1¼" basic, 17 rows.

Bromeliad
(Pink Flame)

*A*long with the lollipop plant, this is one of the flowers that helped me cure my "winter doldrums." I was extremely pleased with the results when visitors who saw the beaded plant alongside the live plant couldn't distinguish them from across the room. Although this pattern is for a full plant, bromeliad flowers provide a striking focal point in a contemporary bouquet.

bromeliad

Materials

- 1 hank bright pink 11/0 seed beads
- 2 hanks medium green 11/0 seed beads
- 1 strand purple 11/0 seed beads
- 26-gauge pink beading wire
- 26-gauge green beading or paddle wire
- 30-gauge assembly wire
- 8"-long 16-gauge stem wire
- ½" green floral tape
- ½" pink floral tape (optional)

Bracts (round top, round bottom)

Make 2 (pink): three-bead basic, seven rows.
Reduce each to one wire and twist.

Make 4 (two pink, two green): three-bead basic, nine rows.
Reduce each to one wire and twist.

Make 4 (pink): three-bead basic, 11 rows.
Reduce each to one wire and twist.

Make 4 (pink): three-bead basic, 13 rows.
Reduce each to one wire and twist.

Make 4 (pink): three-bead basic, 15 rows.
Reduce each to one wire and twist.

Flower (round top, round bottom)

Make 1 (purple) as follows:

1• Leave 3" of bare wire.

2• Make three three-row continuous loops.

3• End with 3" of bare wire, cut from the spool, and twist the wires together.

Leaves (pointed top, round bottom)

Make 4 (green): 3½" basic, five rows.
Reduce each to one wire and twist.

Make 4 (green): 4" basic, five rows.
Reduce each to one wire and twist.

Make 4 (green): 4½" basic, five rows.
Reduce each to one wire and twist.

Make 4 (green): 5" basic, five rows.
Reduce each to one wire and twist.

Detail of bromeliad leaves. Notice how different this leaf is from that of the previous project. The long, thin leaf is created by using a longer basic and fewer rows.

ASSEMBLY

1• Lightly tape the top half of the stem wire with pink floral tape, if available.

2• Use the edge of a ruler, or other slim-edged object, to fold all of the bracts in half lengthwise, toward the back.

3• Fan the flower, position inside one of the folded bracts so that they are just above the top edge, and twist the stem wires together lightly.

4• Use assembly wire to attach the two small, seven-row bracts, with open edges facing each other, to the tip of the stem wire.

5• Slide two nine-row bracts over the small bracts. Position them so that there is ¼" to ½" between their tips and secure with assembly wire.

6• In the same manner as step 5, attach two 11-row bracts.

7• Cut about 6" of beading wire.

8• From the inside, thread the wire through the fold of the lowest bract, at the base of the basic row (Figure 22). Then, thread it around the basic and back through to the inside. Pull the long end to the opposite bract and repeat. Pull the ends together tightly and twist.

9• Attach the remaining bracts, as follows:
- two 13-row
- two 15-row
- two 15-row (thread and tighten)
- two 13-row
- two 11-row

10• Tape over the lower half of the stem with green floral tape.

11• Add the two green nine-row bracts, thread, and tighten.

12• Bead down the stem for 1½".

13• Attach the four small leaves, all at the same level, directly below the beaded area.

14• Attach the rest of the leaves, smallest to largest, with each level directly below the spaces of the previous row.

15• Trim the remaining wires to different lengths, secure them with assembly wire, and cover with green floral tape.

16• Fold the top two thirds of each leaf in half lengthwise.

Lace opposing petals together to keep them stabilized. Work from the insides, to keep everything invisible.

**Figure 22•
Securing the
Bromeliad**

Folding the bracts creates the flat, fanned look of this flower.

Spider
Mum

Materials

- 2½ hanks 11/0 white seed beads
- 4 or more strands 11/0 green beads
- 24- or 26-gauge white or silver beading wire
- 30-gauge assembly wire
- 18"-long 16-gauge stem wire
- ½" green floral tape

Petals (continuous loops)

Make 1 (white) as follows:
1•Leave 2" of bare wire and make nine 2" continuous loops.
2•End with 1" of bare wire, cut from the spool, and twist the entire length.

Make 2 (white) as follows:
1•Leave 2" of bare wire and make seven 3" continuous loops.
2•End with 1" of bare wire, cut from the spool, and twist the entire length.

Make 4 (white) as follows:
1•Leave 2" of bare wire and make eight 4" continuous loops.
2•End with 1" of bare wire, cut from the spool, and twist the entire length.

Make 3 (white) as follows:
1•Leave 2" of bare wire and make eight 5" continuous loops.
2•End with 1" of bare wire, cut from the spool, and twist the entire length.

Make 6 (white) as follows:
1•Leave 2" of bare wire and make eight 6" continuous loops.
2•End with 1" of bare wire, cut from the spool, and twist the entire length.

Leaves (pointed top, pointed bottom)

Make 1 (green): 1" basic, five rows plus four loops.
1•Make rows 1 through 5, as usual.
2•Make a 2" and 1½" loop of beads, on either side of the leaf.
3•Pinch the loops closed and shape them against the side of the leaf.
4•Leave three wires, twist, and lace the loops in place.

Make 1 (green): 2" basic, five rows plus four loops.
1•Make rows 1 through 5, as usual.
2•Make a 4" and 3" loop of beads, on either side of the leaf.
3•Pinch the loops closed and shape them against the side of the leaf.
4•Leave three wires, twist, and lace the loops in place.

While experimenting with "twisted petals," I decided to use them to create something quick and simple. In this case, I choose artistic license over reality. This large flower, often called a football mum, is a wonderful, easy, and versatile flower.

Tip: *This flower is made of groups of twisted loops. When making the loops, measure the beads. Cross the wires below the beads and twist the entire loop. Once the beads are twisted, give the wire at the base an additional twist or two. This will prevent the beads from breaking.*

spider mum

ASSEMBLY

1•Lightly tape the stem wire.

2•Use assembly wire to attach the shortest loop group to the tip of the wire.

3•Attach the rest of the loop groups, smallest to largest. Attach the same sizes at the same level. The one exception is that you will have two rows of the largest size.

4•Using assembly wire, attach the smallest leaf 1½" below the flower and the large leaf 3" below the flower.

5•Use floral tape to wrap the entire stem. Beading the stem is also recommended.

6•Gently curve all of the petals inward and then twirl the stem to separate the petals into a natural position.

Small
Sunflower

Materials

- 1-1/2 hanks yellow, orange, or amber 11/0 seed beads
- ½-hank brown 11/0 seed beads
- 1 hank green 11/0 seed beads
- 24- or 26-gauge gold beading wire
- 24- or 26-gauge green beading or paddle wire
- 30-gauge assembly wire
- 3 18"-long 16-gauge stem wires
- ½" green floral tape

Petals (pointed top, pointed bottom)

Make 24 (yellow): ¾" basic, seven rows*.

1•Reduce each to one wire and twist.
2•Form pairs by twisting the wires of two petals together for ¼", ¼" from the base of the petals, creating 12 pairs.
3•Stack three pairs of petals and twist the wires together, beginning ½" from the last twist, creating four groups.

*To shade the petals as pictured (optional):

1•Cut approximately 24" of wire.
2•Form the basic wire and basic loop on one end of the bare wire.
3•Put ¾" of orange beads on both the basic wire and cut end.
4•Add a few yellow beads to the cut end and complete row 2.
5•On row 3, use enough yellow beads to match the length of yellow on row 2.
6•Add enough orange beads to complete row 3.
7•Continue in the same manner, beginning each odd-numbered row and ending each even-numbered row with ¾" of orange beads.

Center (round)

Make 1 (brown): one-bead basic, 22 rows.

1•Complete rows 1 through 18 as usual. You will be at the top of the center disk.
2•Leave two beads at the top of row 19 and then make a five-bead loop (Figure 23).

Sunflowers appear in many colors and sizes, from daisy-sized red flowers to sunny yellow towering giants. Since you cannot easily use the Large Sunflower (page 114) in many arrangements, I decided a more versatile size was in order. This sunflower looks great in autumn arrangements. The bloom is approximately 4" in diameter.

small sunflower

3•Leave two beads and form another five-bead loop. Continue in this manner until you have approximately 15 loops, as shown (Figure 24).
4•Twist around the bottom wires to complete row 19.
5•Do the same for row 20.
6•For rows 21 and 22, use the same technique, but make approximately 16 loops per row.

(continued)

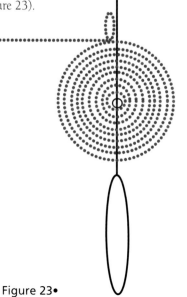

Figure 23•

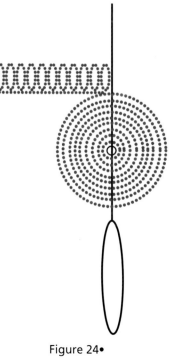

Sunflower Loops •
After row 18, begin making beaded loops.

Figure 24•

7•End at the top of the disk, cut the wire to 3", and twist it with the top basic wire (Figure 25).

8•Cut and twist the bottom basic wire.

9•Bring the two twisted wires together in center at back of the disk and twist.

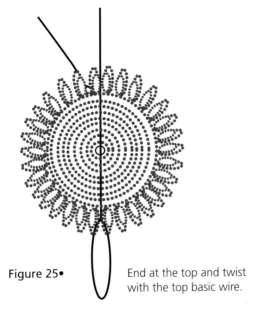

Figure 25•

End at the top and twist with the top basic wire.

Sepals (pointed top, round bottom)
Make 10 (green): ¼" basic, 11 rows.
Reduce each to one wire and twist.

Leaves (pointed top, round bottom)
Make 2 (green): ¼" basic, 25 rows.

1•Leave three wires, twist, and tape.

2•Lace once across the center.

The leaf is ¼" basic, 11 rows. The stem is beaded, which adds both strength and beauty to the finished piece.

ASSEMBLY

1• Use assembly wire to firmly bind the three stem wires together.

2• Lightly cover them with floral tape.

3• Use assembly wire to attach the center disk to the top of the stem. Position it so that the stem wire "just" touches the back of the disk.

4• Hold a petal group against the stem wire. Attach it so that the petals extend beyond the disk, as shown in Figure 26, with no stem wire showing.

5• Secure the other three groups in the same manner.

6• Directly below the petals, secure five sepals, wrong-side-up, spaced evenly around the stem.

7• Position and secure the remaining sepals directly below and between those secured in step 6.

8• Cut all of the exposed wires to different lengths and secure tightly with assembly wire.

9• Bend all of the sepals upward so that their tips are resting on the bottoms of the petals.

10• Attach the leaves at attractive heights.

11• Cover the entire stem with floral tape. Beading the stem is recommended.

12•Spread the petals and pull them into several attractive layers.

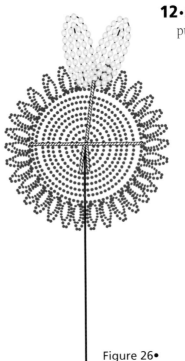

Figure 26•
Leaf Positioning

Notice what a different look shading creates on the sunflower below compared to the one above.

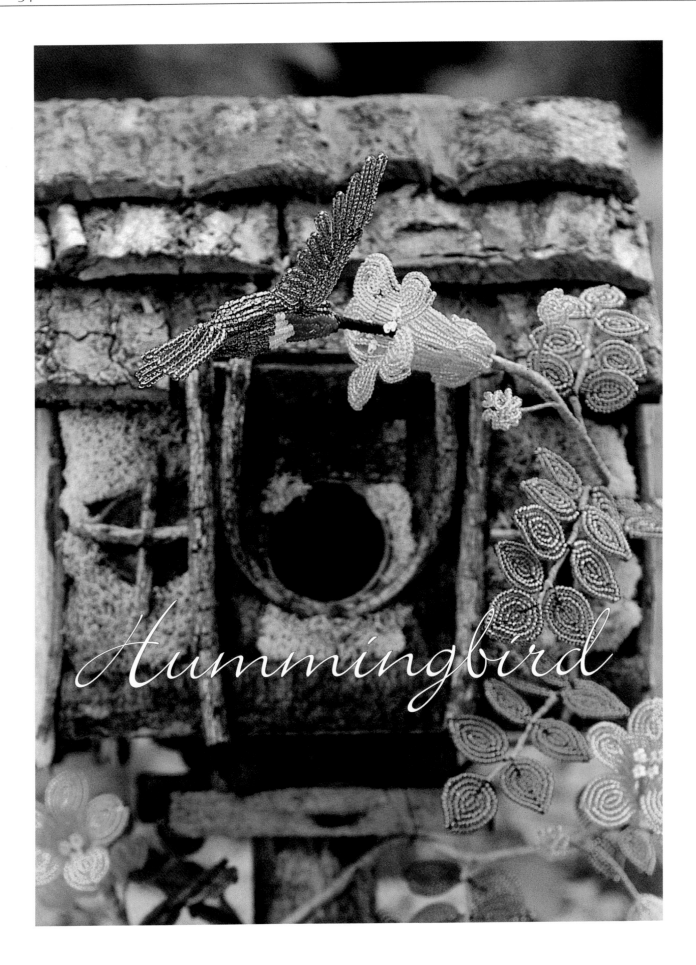

Hummingbird

Materials

- 4 strands iridescent or copper-lined green 11/0 seed beads
- 3 strands gray or silver 11/0 seed beads
- ½-strand white 11/0 seed beads
- ½-strand red 11/0 seed beads
- 24- or 26-gauge green beading or paddle wire
- 30-gauge green lacing wire (lacing and assembly)
- 18"-long 16-gauge stem wire
- Black floss and/or black floral tape
- Krazy Glue (optional)
- 2 round, black ⅛" disks or beads (optional; for eyes)

My husband and I are amateur bird watchers. Even though I did try to resist, I finally gave in to the pressure and created a hummingbird for him. Of course, now he wants cardinals and bluebirds, too! I hope you enjoy this little guy and appreciate the uniqueness he brings to your arrangements.

hummingbird

Belly (slightly pointed top, slightly pointed bottom)
Make 1 as follows:

1•Cut approximately 3 feet of beading wire.

2•Form a regular basic wire and basic loop.

3•Working one row at a time, add beads in the sequence that follows, remembering that you may have to add or subtract to accommodate your "style" and still maintain the pattern (Figure 27).

Row 1: (basic row) four red, six white, 10 green

Row 2: six red, six white, 10 green

Row 3: 11 green, five white, eight red

Row 4: 11 red, five white, 14 green

Row 5: 18 green, four white, 12 red

Row 6: 17 red, three white, 18 green

Row 7: 21 green, three white, 15 red

Row 8: 20 red, two white, 21 green

Row 9: 25 green, two white, 20 red

4•Do not cut the top basic wire.

5•Reduce bottom to one wire and twist.

Back and Tail (slightly pointed top, slightly pointed bottom)
Make 1 (green/gray): 1⅛" basic, 15 rows.

1•Complete rows 1 through 3 as usual and then after completing row 3, bend the basic loop backwards 45 degrees (Figure 28).

2•Proceed through row 13.

3•For row 14, measure enough green beads to complete the row ½" short of the top basic wire.

4•Measure another 24" of bare wire and cut from spool.

5•Add 2" of gray beads and make a loop, using only the gray.

6•Add two green beads and 1¾" of gray beads and make a loop, using only the gray.

7•Add two green beads and 1½" of gray beads and make a loop, using only the gray. (This should finish the row. If not, move on to the next loop and then finish the row).

8•Add two green beads and 1¼" of gray beads and make a loop, using only the gray.

9•Add two green beads and 1½" of gray beads and make a loop, using only the gray.

10•Add two green beads and 1¾" of gray beads and make a loop, using only the gray.

11•Add two green beads and 2" of gray beads and make a loop, using only the gray.

12•Add enough green beads to complete the row, reduce to one wire, and twist.

13•Do not cut the top basic wire.

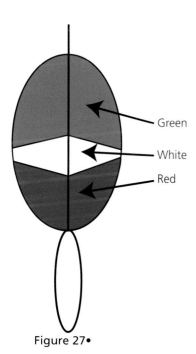

Green

White

Red

Figure 27•

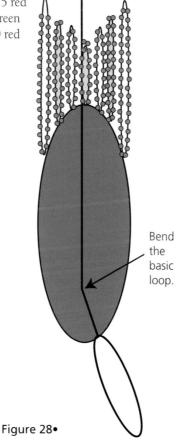

Bend the basic loop.

Figure 28•

(continued)

Wings (round top, round bottom)

Make 2 (green and gray): 1" basic, five rows (green with gray loops)

1•Complete rows 1 through 3 as usual.

2•Measure 24" of bare wire and cut from spool.

3•For row 4, make the wing feathers using the same method used on the tail with two green beads spaced between measured loops of gray beads in the following pattern:

Loop 1: Add two green beads and 1" of gray beads and make a loop, using only the gray.

Loop 2: Add two green beads and 1⅛" of gray beads and make a loop, using only the gray.

Loop 3: Add two green beads and 1¼" gray and make a loop, using only the gray.

Loop 4: Add two green beads and 1⅜" gray and make a loop, using only the gray.

Loop 5: Add two green beads and 1½" gray and make a loop, using only the gray.

Loop 6: Add two green beads and 1⅝" gray and make a loop, using only the gray.

Loop 7: Add two green beads and 1¾" gray and make a loop, using only the gray.

Loop 8: Add two green beads and 1⅞" gray and make a loop, using only the gray.

Loop 9: Add two green beads and 2" gray and make a loop, using only the gray.

Loop 10: Add two green beads and 2⅛" gray and make a loop, using only the gray. Complete the row.

4•For row 5, use all green beads.

5•Leave three wires, twist, and lace the wing across the green portion only (Figure 29).

Figure 29•
Hummingbird Wing

Detail of finished hummingbird wing. Notice how the gray "feathers" are seemlessly incorporated into the outside band of green wing beads, just as the pattern steps instruct.

ASSEMBLY

1•Leaving a 2" "tail" of lacing wire on both sides, lace the belly piece once across the red portion and once across the green portion. Trim the belly stem to 1¼".

2•Hold the belly with right-side facing you. Gently curve the red portion toward you and the green portion backwards.

3•Shape the back-and-tail piece and hold it against the belly. Note the position where the lacing wires of the belly meet the edges of the back-and-tail piece, as shown (Figure 30). Set the belly aside.

4•Leaving a 2" "tail" of lacing wire, lace the back-and-tail piece at both places where it had matched up to the lacing wires on the belly piece. Lace once across the tail. Trim the stem to 1¼".

5•Again, using the belly piece to measure, determine how far apart the wings should be and twist them together. Note: The bottom beads of the wings, when spread apart, should touch the outer edges of the "red-meets-white" portion of the belly, as shown (Figure 31).

6•Trim the twisted wing wires to ½".

7•With the cut wires and the "feathers" facing upward toward the tip, use assembly wire to securely attach the wings to the top ½" of the stem wire. Optional: Put a drop of glue on the assembly area and set aside to dry.

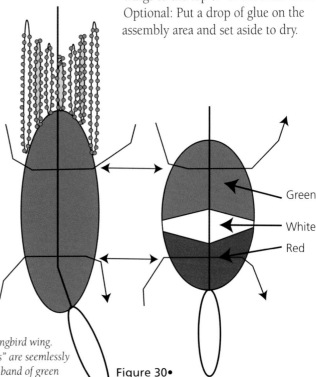

Green
White
Red

Figure 30•
Match the Levels of Lacing

8• With wrong sides up and positioned tip-to-tip, match the top basic wire of the belly to the top basic wire of the back-and-tail piece. Twist the top basic wires together and trim to ½".

9• Gently fold the body portions closed over the wings.

10• Position the body so that the wings are at the "red-meets-white" portion on the body.

11• Use assembly wire to securely attach the wires of the body parts to the stem. If this is bulky, trim the wires so that they will lay flat against the stem. Optional: Put a drop of glue on the assembly area and set aside to dry.

12• Twist the corresponding "tails" of lacing wire together to lash the sides closed. Trim the twisted lacing wires to ½" and tuck them inside the body.

13• Position and attach eyes, if desired.

14• Use black floral tape and floss to cover the 1¼" of the assembly area.

15• Place a slight bend at the end of the bird's "beak" and position his wings.

16• To keep him "fed," assemble and attach your favorite flower on the same stem, just below the tip of his beak.

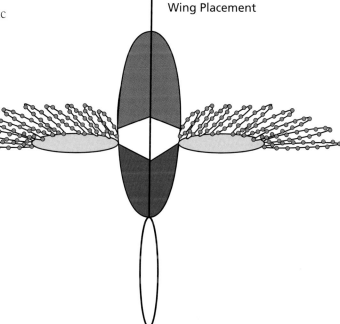

Figure 31•
Wing Placement

Close-up of finished hummingbird head. The creation of a three-dimensional piece is accomplished through careful planning of how individual pieces match up before lacing them

Trumpet Vine

Materials

- ½-hank orange 11/0 seed beads
- ½-hank light green 11/0 seed beads
- 20 white 11/0 seed beads
- 26-gauge gold beading wire
- 26-gauge green beading or paddle wire
- 30-gauge gold wire (lacing and assembly)
- 18"-long 16-gauge stem wire
- Green floral tape

Petals (pointed top, round bottom)

Make 5 (orange): three-bead basic, nine rows.
1. Begin each with a 3½" basic wire and a small basic loop.
2. After row 3, add eight beads to the top basic wire and complete rows 4 and 5.
3. Pinch the rows tight against the basic row.
4. In the same manner, add eight beads to the top basic wire after both rows 6 and 7.
5. Pinch all of the rows tight.
6. Leave the top basic wire as is.
7. Twist the bottom wires, trim to ¼", and fold them back against the reverse side of the petal.

Sepals and Buds (loops)

Make 2 (orange) as follows:
1. Leave 3" of bare wire.
2. Using 1½" of beads for the first loops, make five continuous three-row crossover loops.
3. End with 3" of bare wire and cut from spool. Do not twist ends together.

Make 1 (orange) as follows:
1. Leave 3" of bare wire.
2. Using 1" of beads for the first loops, make five continuous loops.
3. End with 3" of bare wire and cut from spool. Do not twist ends together.

Stamens (loops)

Make 2 (white) as follows:
1. Cut 7" of bare wire.
2. Place 10 white beads on the wire and make two five-bead loops in the center of the wire.
3. Fold in half and twist.

Pistil

Make 1 (green) as follows:
1. Cut 7" of bare wire.
2. Place one green bead in the center of the wire.
3. Fold in half and twist.

Leaves (pointed top, round bottom):

Make 7 (green): three-bead basic, seven rows.
Reduce to one wire and twist.
Make 9 (green): three-bead basic, nine rows
Reduce to one wire and twist.

(continued)

Not only is this vine a beautiful little flower on its own, but it also makes a perfect companion to the hummingbird. If you do choose to add a hummingbird, however, make the hummingbird before assembling the flower.

trumpet vine

Detail of the inside of the trumpet vine flower.

ASSEMBLY

For the flowers:

1• Lightly tape the stem wire.

2• Leave a slight 2" "tail" and in one continuous motion, lace all of the petals together, just over row 3 (Figure 32).

3• Bring the ends of the lacing wire together, with the right sides of the petals facing inward.

4• Twist the lacing wires together, cut to ¼", and hide ends between rows.

5• With 1½" extending beyond the tip, use assembly wire to attach the pistil and stamen to the top of the stem wire.

6• Position the flower over the stamens and pistil and secure it to the stem wire.

7• Wrap one of the large sepals around the base of the flower, making sure it is pointing upward, with the wrong side against the flower. Use assembly wire to secure.

8• Use floral tape to cover the 1" closest to the flower.

9• Trim the remaining wires to different lengths.

10• Curve the loops of the two remaining sepals inward and shape to form buds. Twist the wires and tape the top 1" of each.

11• Use assembly wire to attach the two buds at the same level as the flower, matching the bottoms of the taped areas.

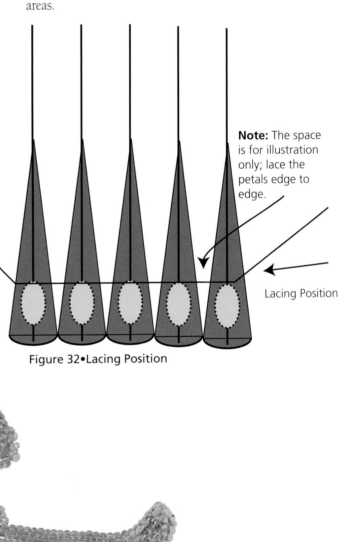

Note: The space is for illustration only; lace the petals edge to edge.

Lacing Position

Figure 32•Lacing Position

For the leaf groups:

1•Using the small leaves, hold two leaves with their bases touching. Position a third leaf so that it extends $1/4$" above the others and twist all three wires for $1/2$".

2•Add two more small leaves to the grouping of step 1 below the first two and twist for $1/2$".

3•Add the last two small leaves below the previous two and twist the remaining wires all the way down.

4•Use floral tape, cut in half lengthwise, to cover the stem from the top leaf to $1/2$" below the bottom pair, as shown (Figure 33).

5•Repeat steps 1 through 4 for the large leaf group, using all nine leaves.

6•Attach the small leaf group at the same level as the flowers.

7•Attach the large leaf group $1^1/2$" down the stem.

8•Cover all assembly areas with floral tape.

9•Bend the tips of the petals outward.

Note: If adding a hummingbird, begin assembling the flower on the beak stem about $2^1/2$" from the bird's head.

Figure 33•
Leaf Position

No stems showing
on side leaflets.

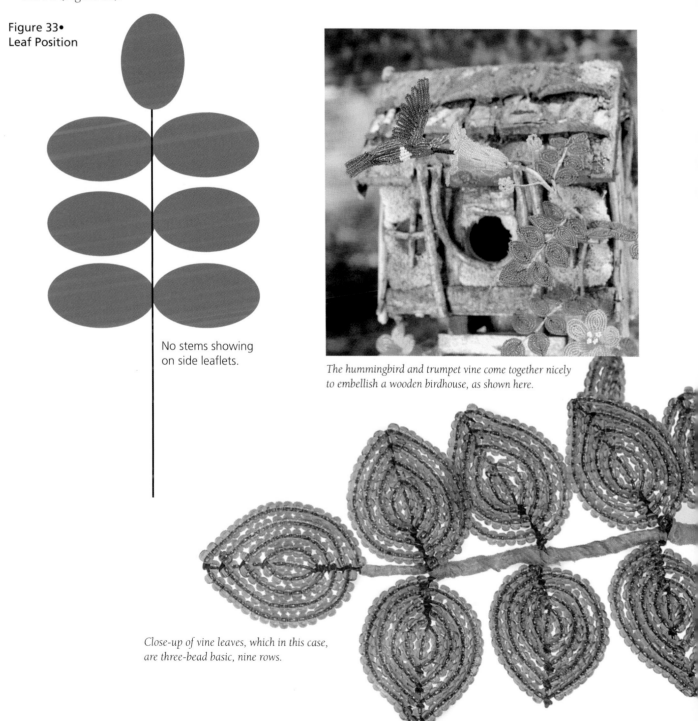

The hummingbird and trumpet vine come together nicely to embellish a wooden birdhouse, as shown here.

Close-up of vine leaves, which in this case, are three-bead basic, nine rows.

Bougainvillea

Materials

- 1 hank pink 11/0 seed beads
- 1 strand white or cream-colored 11/0 seed beads
- 9 yellow 11/0 or 10/0 seed beads
- ½-hank green 11/0 seed beads
- 24- or 26-gauge petal-colored beading wire
- 26-gauge green beading or paddle wire
- 30-gauge wire (assembly)
- 18"-long 16-gauge stem wire
- ½" green floral tape

Bracts (pointed top, round bottom)
Make 18 (pink): four-bead basic, 13 rows.
Leave three wires and twist for each.

Flowers (continuous loops)
Make 9 (white or cream) as follows:
1•Leave 4" of bare wire.
2•Using seven beads per loop, make five continuous loops.
3•End with 4" of bare wire and cut from the spool.
4•Bring one of the cut wires to the top of the petal loops, add a yellow bead, and center the bead in the middle of the petals.
5•Bring the wire back to the bottom.
6•Twist the two wires together.

Buds (crossover loops)
Make 9 (white or cream) as follows:
1•Leave 4" of bare wire.
2•Using eight beads for the first loop, make one four-row crossover loop.
3•End with 4" of bare wire and cut from spool.
4•Twist the wires together.

Leaves (pointed top, round bottom)
Make 5 (green): eight-bead basic, 17 rows.
On each, leave three wires, twist and lace.

Detail of bougainvillea flower with its pink bracts (four-bead basic, 13 rows) and white flowers (continuous loops).

After my first visit to Yuma, Arizona, I fell in love with this wonderful flower bush. Even in the scorching desert sun, mounds and mounds of colored bracts can be seen hanging over every garden wall. It is difficult to get the "crepe paper" look with beads, but this is still an adorable flower. Choose pink, red, white, or lemon yellow beads for a natural look.

bougainvillea

ASSEMBLY

1• Lightly tape the stem wire.

2• Holding three flowers and/or buds together (mix and match), twist the lower stems together tightly 1" from the beads. Repeat for all six groups.

3• Use assembly wire to attach three bracts to each flower group 1¼" below the flower tops.

4• Use floral tape, cut in half lengthwise, to cover the top 2" of the flower/bract stems.

5• Use the same size floral tape to cover the top 1" of each leaf stem.

6• Thin the unwrapped flower/bract stem wires by cutting the wires to different lengths.

7• Use assembly wire to attach one flower/bract to the tip of the stem wire.

8• Add two more flowers/bracts ¼" below the first.

9• Wrap the assembly wire down ½" and add one flower/bract and two leaves.

10• Go down another ½" and secure two more flowers/ bracts plus one leaf.

11• Position the final two leaves at an attractive level and secure.

12• Cover the entire stem and all construction areas with floral tape.

13• Push all of the bracts upward around the flowers.

Peony

Materials

- 2 hanks red, pink, or white 11/0 seed beads
- ½-hank medium or dark green 11/0 seed beads
- 24-gauge petal-colored beading wire
- 26-gauge green paddle wire (greenery)
- 30-gauge petal-colored wire (lacing)
- 30-gauge assembly wire
- 18"-long 16-gauge stem wire
- ½" green floral tape

Center Petals (12 continuous loop variations and six round top, round bottom)

Make 1 (red, pink, or white) as follows:

1•Leave 3" of bare wire.
2•Make 12 continuous loops, using 1" of beads per loop.
3•End with 3" of bare wire.
4•Cut from spool and twist the wires together.

Make 3 (red, pink, or white) as follows:

1•Leave 3" of bare wire.
2•Make six continuous loops, using 1½" of beads per loop.
3•End with 3" of bare wire.
4•Cut from spool and twist the wires together.
5•To create a petal, lace the loops together ¼" from the tips.

Make 4 (red, pink, or white) as follows:

1•Leave 3" of bare wire.
2•Make six continuous loops, using 2" of beads per loop.
3•End with 3" of bare wire.
4•Cut from spool and twist the wires.
5•To create a petal, lace the loops together ¼" from the tips.

Make 4 (red, pink, or white) as follows:

1•Leave 3" of bare wire.
2•Make 12 continuous loops, using 2½" of beads per loop.
3•End with 3" of bare wire.
4•Cut from spool and twist the wires. When twisting, the petal may buckle, but don't be concerned. This will not show, and in fact, it adds depth to the flower.
5•To create a petal, lace the loops together, ¼" from the tips.

Make 6 (red, pink, or white): two-bead basic, 19 rows.

Reduce each to one wire, twist, and lace.

Sepals

Make 2 (green; round top, round bottom): one-bead basic, 13 rows.

Reduce each to one wire and twist.

Make 2 (green; pointed top, round bottom): ½" basic, five rows.

1•After completing row 5, make loops on either side of the petal, using 2½" of beads per loop, as shown (Figure 34).
2•Reduce to one wire and twist.
3•Pinch the loops closed.

As I walked through our garden, surrounded by huge, showy peonies, I decided that the smallest of the varieties would be my model for this pattern. You, however, are not required to follow my example. To increase the size, add additional rows to the bottom petals or simply add more, progressively larger, petals.

peony

Leaves (pointed top, pointed bottom)

Make 1 (green): 1" basic, 13 rows.

Reduce to one wire, twist, and lace.

Make 1 (green): 1" basic, 17 rows.

Reduce to one wire, twist, and lace.

(continued)

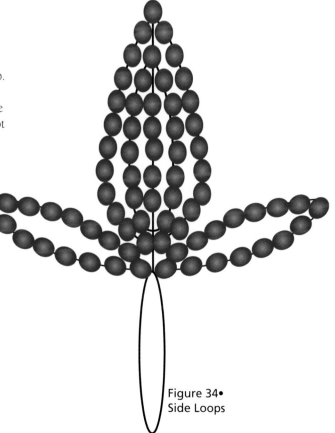

Figure 34•
Side Loops

ASSEMBLY

(The peony is assembled in the same manner as a rose.)

1•Lightly tape the stem wire.

2•Use assembly wire to attach the unlaced group of small loops to the end of the stem.

3•Continue attaching the loop petals, smallest to largest, securing the petals of the same size at the same level.

4•Add three round petals directly below the largest loop petals and then add the last three round petals.

5•As close to the flower as possible and opposite each other, secure the two round sepals, with wrong sides facing upward.

6•In the spaces between the round sepals, add the last two sepals, with the wrong sides facing downward.

7•Pull the remaining wires away from the stem and cut them all to different lengths.

8•Smooth the wires back down and continue wrapping them in place with the assembly wire.

9•Beginning with the smallest first, add the two leaves at attractive levels on the stem.

10•Use floral tape to cover the stem, paying special attention to the area directly below the flower.

11•Slightly curl the pointed sepals and loops downward.

Detail of finished red peony. Notice what an interesting effect is created by combining continuous loop petals with round top, round bottom petals, all using the same color beads.

Materials

- 1 hank copper-lined light green 11/0 seed beads
- 26-gauge green beading or paddle wire
- 30-gauge paddle wire (assembly)
- 18"-long 16-gauge stem wire
- ½" green floral tape

Leaves (round top, round bottom)

Make 2 (green): one-bead basic, nine rows.
  Reduce each to one wire.

Make 2 (green): one-bead basic, 11 rows.
  Reduce each to one wire.

Make 2 (green): one-bead basic, 13 rows.
  Reduce each to one wire.

Make 14 (green): one-bead basic, 15 rows.
  Reduce each to one wire.

ASSEMBLY

1· Lightly tape the stem wire.

2· Using assembly wire, attach the pair of small leaves to the tip of the stem wire.

3· Add the next largest set of leaves ½" below and at a 90-degree angle from the first.

4· Add the next largest set of leaves ¼" below and at a 90-degree angle from the second.

5· Drop down 1" and add the rest of the leaves at 1" intervals in the same manner.

6· Use floral tape to cover the entire stem again.

Beginning with a one-bead basic allows you to create a leaf that is more round than oblong.

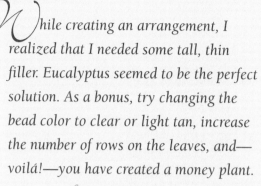

While creating an arrangement, I realized that I needed some tall, thin filler. Eucalyptus seemed to be the perfect solution. As a bonus, try changing the bead color to clear or light tan, increase the number of rows on the leaves, and— voilá!—you have created a money plant.

eucalyptus stems

Eucalyptus Stems

Dendrobium Orchid

Materials

- ⅔-hank petal-colored 11/0 seed beads
- 32 white 11/0 seed beads
- 24- or 26-gauge colored beading wire
- 30-gauge wire (lacing and assembly)
- 18"-long 16-gauge stem wire
- ½" floral tape

Petals (pointed top, round bottom)

Make 4 (petal color): ¾" basic, five rows. These are the "center top" petals.

1 • Reduce to one wire and leave the bottom wires of four petals untwisted.

2 • On these four petals, put eight white beads on the bottom wire.

3 • Form a single loop at the base of the petal.

4 • Twist the wires and set aside.

Make 40 (petal color): ¾" basic, five rows. These are the "small" petals.

Reduce each to one wire and twist.

Make 4 (petal color): 1" basic, five rows. These are the "large" petals.

Reduce each to one wire and twist.

Make 4 (petal color): ¾" basic, three rows. These are the "lip" petals.

1 • After completing row 3, begin with ¾" of beads and make a double-loop on the right and another on the left side of the petal.

2 • Shape the loops so that they form "sides" on the petal.

3 • Cut 5" of lacing wire.

4 • Attach the lacing wire to the lower edge of one of the outer loops.

5 • Lace the wire through the petal twice. Do not cut.

6 • Place four petal-colored beads on the lacing wire.

7 • Skipping three beads on the petal, lace the wire around the petal, and then through the ruffle just completed. Pull tight. This is the same process as that shown in Figure 37 of the Cattleya Orchid instructions, page 57.

8 • Add another four petal-colored beads to the wire and continue to make ruffles around the petal until you reach the loop on the other side (five to seven ruffles total).

9 • Lace twice around the lower-outside row of the loop and cut the lacing wire (Figure 35).

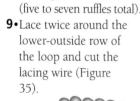

Figure 35•
Petal with
Ruffle Loops

This spray of small orchids is ideal alone or in a bouquet. This pattern makes four blooms, or approximately 7" of flowers. For longer stems, simply continue to add flowers. As with almost any orchid, you can choose your colors at will.

dendrobium orchid

ASSEMBLY

1 • Lightly tape the stem wire and set it aside.

2 • Position a small petal on either side of a lip petal. Twist the wires together lightly.

3 • Position a large petal on either side of a "center top" petal. Twist the wires together lightly.

4 • Hold the two pieces together so that the loop on the center top petal fits into the trough of the lip petal. Twist the pieces together tightly.

5 • Use floral tape to wrap the top 1½" of the twisted stem, nearest to the flower.

6 • Set this aside and complete the other three flowers in the same manner.

7 • Position the top flower so that it extends 1¼" above the top of the stem wire.

8 • Use assembly wire to secure it in place.

9 • Continue to secure the remaining flowers at 1½" intervals down the stem wire.

10 • Use floral tape to cover the entire stem again.

11 • Twist the beads of the center top petal one quarter-turn to the left.

12 • Flare the two large petals out and back.

Detail of dendrobium orchid. As you can see, the various petal sizes come together seamlessly.

Spiderwort

Materials

- 1 strand petal-colored 11/0 seed beads
- 2 strands green 11/0 seed beads
- 6 yellow 11/0 seed beads
- 24- or 26-gauge colored beading wire
- 24- or 26-gauge green beading or paddle wire
- 30-gauge gold wire (assembly)
- 6 18"-long 16-gauge stem wire
- ½" green floral tape

Petals (pointed top, round bottom)
Make 3 (petal color): four-bead basic, seven rows.
Reduce each to one wire.

Stamens (continuous loops)
Make 1 (yellow beads on 30-gauge wire) as follows:
1•Leave 3" of bare wire.
2•Make six twisted continuous loops, containing one yellow bead each.
3•End with 3" of bare wire, cut from spool, and twist the wires together.

Buds (crossover loops)
Make 2 (one green, one petal color) as follows:
1•Leave 3" of bare wire.
2•Make a 16-bead loop with two crossover loops.
3•End with 3" of bare wire and cut from spool.
4•Twist the wires and tape the top 1½".
Make 2* (green) as follows:
1•Leave 3" of bare wire.
2•Make a 12-bead crossover loop.
3•End with 3" of bare wire and cut from spool.
4•Twist the wires and tape the top 1½".
*You need at least two of this variation, but you may do more, if desired.

Leaf (pointed top, round bottom)
Make 1 (green): 3" basic, seven rows.
Leave three wires, lace, and twist.

ASSEMBLY

1• Lightly tape the stem wire.

2• Hold all three petals and the stamen together.

3• Twist all of the bottom wires together tightly.

4• Use floral tape to cover 1½" of the twisted wires, closest to the flower.

5• Hold the flowers and buds together, with the top of the buds at different levels and slightly lower than the flower.

Although this small flower seems unimpressive on its own, it is a wonderful filler for bouquets. In nature, the flowers can be found in white, pink, or blue.

spiderwort

Detail of finished spiderwort, which is a delicate flower of just three petals with a cluster of continuous-looped stamens.

6• Allowing 1" of the flower stem to rise above the taped stem wire, use 30-gauge wire to attach them securely.

7• Directly below the flowers you attached in step 6, attach the leaf so that its base touches the stem.

8• Taper the wire lengths and re-tape the entire stem.

9• Pinch the base of the leaf around the stem wire and crease it down the center.

Plumeria

Materials

- 1 hank white 11/0 seed beads
- 3 strands yellow 11/0 seed beads
- ½-hank red 11/0 seed beads
- 2 hanks light or medium green 11/0 seed beads
- ½-hank brown 11/0 seed beads
- 2 strands tan 10/0 or 11/0 seed beads
- 24- or 26-gauge white, red, and green beading wire
- 30-gauge lacing wire
- 28-gauge wire (assembly and stem beading)
- 5 18"-long 16-gauge stem wires
- 2 18"-long 20-gauge stem wires, cut in half
- ½" green floral tape

Once described as "antlers wearing posies," this tropical flower is a real beauty. Though the basic construction of most specimens is quite similar, I have tried to add a few suggestions for making an assortment of shapes and colors. You may find it helpful to read the variations before buying beads.

plumeria

Petals (slightly pointed top, round bottom)
Make 10 (yellow and white): 12-bead basic, 15 rows.
  1•Cut 36" of beading wire.
  2•Form a normal basic wire and loop without beads.
  3•Use six yellow beads below six white beads for the basic row.
  4•Begin each even-numbered row and end each odd-numbered row with six yellow beads.
  5•Reduce to one wire and lace all.

Buds (round top, round bottom)
Make 2 (white): 12-bead basic, 15 rows.
  Leave three wires and twist.
Make 3 (red): 1¼" basic, 17 rows.
  Leave three wires and twist.

Leaves (pointed top, pointed bottom)
Make 4 (green): 4" basic, 17 rows.
  1•Use a 9" piece of 20-gauge stem wire held against the back of the original basic row during construction to stiffen the leaf, as in Stem Stiffening Option 1, page 16.
  2•Leave three wires and twist.

(continued)

Detail of plumeria flower, which utilizes several different techniques to achieve the finished tropical splendor. Note the shading on the petals, the interesting look of the twisted buds, and the beading on the stems.

Variations

- Flowers are also found in solid pink or solid yellow, as well as with varied sizes of the yellow center.
- To vary the size of the center, you may reduce the number of yellow beads down to three per row, or as high as 12 per row.
- You may also shade the yellow portion with the darkest beads at the bottom.
- Petal shapes may be altered by making a pointed top, pointed bottom or a round top, round bottom.
- Buds may also be completed using only the petal color.

ASSEMBLY

1• Lightly tape all stem wires.

2• Use assembly wire to attach five white flower petals to the very tip of a stem wire. Allow the petals to overlap with one side above and one side below its neighbor.

3• Use green beads on wire to wrap the top 5" of the stem.

4• Set aside and repeat for the second flower.

5• For each of the two buds, lay one white petal against a red petal.

6• Twist the petals into a spiral.

7• Twist the last red petal into a spiral.

8• Attach each bud to the tip of a separate stem wire.

9• Use green beads on wire to wrap the top 5" of each stem.

10• For the leaves, use green beads on wire to wrap the top 1¹/₂" of the stem.

11• Use 28-gauge wire to bind the two flowers together as close to the beaded area as possible.

12• Add the three buds and four leaves in the same manner.

13• Continue wrapping the wire down the unbeaded bundle of stems.

14• String the brown and tan beads onto a spool of wire, beginning with 1" of tan followed by 4" to 6" of brown. Repeat this proportion until you have at least 6 feet of strung beads.

15• Use the brown-and-tan beaded wire to wrap the lower stem, stopping 3" from the bottom.

16• Cover the exposed wire with floral tape.

17• Cup the flower petals toward the top and slightly twist them into a "swirl."

The long lines of the plumeria leaf are achieved with a 4" basic, 17 rows wide.

Shown here is the plumeria in an arrangement with violets. The violet pattern is detailed in my first book, French-Beaded Flowers: New Millennium Collection *(see Resources, page 126).*

Cattleya
Orchid

This large, beautiful flower looks lovely without a bouquet. Therefore, I have designed it as a table piece. It has its own built-in stand. Although the pattern calls for white beads, the flower pictured was made by using clear beads. Most of the petals are on white wire, but the lip petal is made using gold wire. The result gives the flower slight shading that the observer can see, but cannot quite define.

cattleya orchid

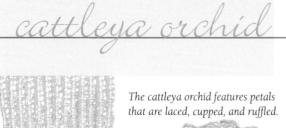

The cattleya orchid features petals that are laced, cupped, and ruffled.

Materials

- 2¼ hanks white 11/0 seed beads
- 1 strand contrasting color 11/0 seed beads (optional)
- 4 black or brown 11/0 seed beads
- 24-gauge white beading wire
- 30-gauge wire (ruffles and assembly)
- 22-gauge white wire, to stiffen petals
- 18"-long 16-gauge stem wire
- ½" white or green floral tape

Sepal Petals (pointed top, round bottom)
Make 3 (white): 2" basic, 13 rows.
  1•Leave three wires and twist.
  2•Lace all petals across the centers.

Side Petals (pointed top, round bottom)
Make 2 (white): 1" basic, 27 rows.
  1•Leave three wires and twist.
  2•Use Stem Stiffening Option 2, page 16, to stiffen stems.
  3•Referring to the ruffle instructions below, sew a single row of ruffles around the entire edge.
  4•Lace each petal across its center.

Lip Petal (round top, round bottom)
Make 1 (white): ³/₄" basic, 43 rows.
  1•Leave three wires and twist.
  2•Use Stem Stiffening Option 2, page 16, to stiffen the stem.
  3•Referring to the ruffle instructions below, sew a double row of ruffles around the entire edge.
  4•Lace the petal twice, as shown (Figure 36).

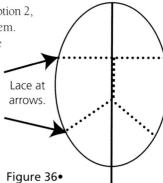

Lace at arrows.

**Figure 36•
Lacing Positions**

Stamen (round top, round bottom)
Make 1 (contrasting color):
1" basic, seven rows.
  1•Complete rows 1 through 3.
  2•Measure 9" of bare wire and cut from spool.
  3• Bend both basic wires backward 90 degrees. Your rows will now form a "beehive." Refer to the Beehive (Cup) section, page 19, for help with this step, if necessary.
  4•Add enough beads to be two beads short of completing the row.
  5•Add one black bead and one contrasting colored bead to complete row 4.
  6•Add one contrasting bead, one black bead, and enough contrasting beads to complete row 5.

7•Add enough beads so that you are three beads short of completing row 6.

8•Add one black bead and two contrasting colored beads to complete row 6.

9•Add two contrasting beads, one black bead, and the contrasting beads to complete row 7.

10•Reduce to two wires and twist.

Ruffles

1•Using 30-gauge wire, cut a piece that is at least four times the circumference of your petal. As close to the beads as possible, wind the wire once around the stem wire. Leave a 1" tail.

2•Threading around the outer row of beads, secure the wire next to the stem.

3•Place five beads on the wire. Skip four beads on the row and wind the wire, front to back, around the row, as shown (Figure 37). Pull the wire tight.

4•Thread the wire through the newly formed loop, front to back. Position the wire so it will fall in the same place. Pull it tight.

5•Bring the wire back to the front, put five beads on it, and repeat steps 3 and 4 until you have gone completely around the petal.

6•When you are finished, twist and trim the end wires.

Note: To add a second row, do it in the same manner, attaching in the same place as the first row (just as if the first row were not there); however, use six beads per loop.

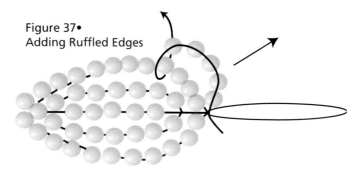

Figure 37•
Adding Ruffled Edges

ASSEMBLY

1• Lightly fold the 16-gauge stem wire in half.

2• Holding the cut ends together, use floral tape to lightly tape the top 3" only.

3• Roll the lip petal into a cone. Pinch the edges of the base (stem end) together so that the ruffles are both facing upward.

4• Slip the stamen inside and position it so that the base of the stamen lies $1/2$" inside the cone. Twist the wires together. The stem of the stamen should not show, as it is inside the pinched area.

5• Using assembly wire, tightly attach the lip to the taped, folded stem wire.

6• Attach the two ruffled side petals as close to the lip as possible.

7• Add the three sepal petals, one at the top and two at the bottom.

8• Cut all of the exposed wires to different lengths (2" and less) and wrap them tightly against the stem with assembly wire.

9• Lightly tape the construction area.

10• Bead $2\frac{1}{2}$" to 3" of the stem by securing the beaded wire to the top of the stem, pushing the beads forward, and wrapping the beaded wire down the stem.

11• Remove any tape and wires that extend below the beads.

12• Slightly bend the doubled stem at the base of the beads.

13• Referring to Figure 38, open the bottom loop to form a circle. Push the side of the circle, where the bend was, toward the flower. This will form a "W" shape that will act as the two legs of the stand. Shape and adjust until the orchid is stable and displayed at an attractive level. Roll the end of the lip down and back.

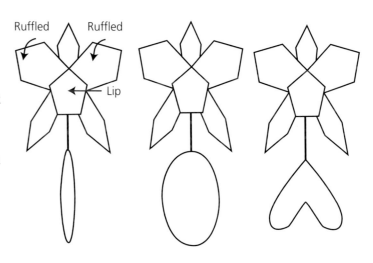

Figure 38•Orchid Stand Assembly

Golden
Grain

Materials

- 2 or 3 strands gold*, tan, or green 11/0 seed beads
- 24-gauge gold wire
- 30-gauge gold wire (assembly)

  *The picture shown is made with two strands of beads. If you would like a longer seed head, simply make more seeds and assemble in the same manner.

Seeds (loops)

Make 25 (gold, tan, or green) as follows:

1•After stringing the beads, leave 1" of bare wire. (This is the stem end.)
2•Make a single loop using 1" of beads.
3•Twist the wire closed, using a full one-and-a-half twist, tight against the beads.
4•Lightly pinch the loop closed.
5•Measure enough beads to go up the front of the loop, as if you were making a three-row crossover loop (Figure 39-A).
6•Measure an extra 2½" of bare wire and cut it from the spool (Figure 39-B).
7•From back to front, thread the 2½" bare wire through the loop, as shown (Figure 39-C).
8•Using pliers, pull the wire tight and up toward the top (Figure 39-D).

This golden seed head will add a touch of elegance to any display. For a fun variation, you can try it in green-and-gold, as I did, for wheat that has not yet ripened.

golden grain

Stem

Make 1 (gold wire) as follows:

1•Cut seven 36"-long pieces of gold wire.
2•Holding the wires together, fold them in half.
3•Loop the fold over a stable object. (A nail placed in a board works well.)
4•Using a pair of locking pliers or hemostats, clamp the cut ends, tug firmly, and smoothly twist the wire to form a tight coil. This twisting can also be done by clamping the cut ends and using a slow-speed electric drill.

(continued)

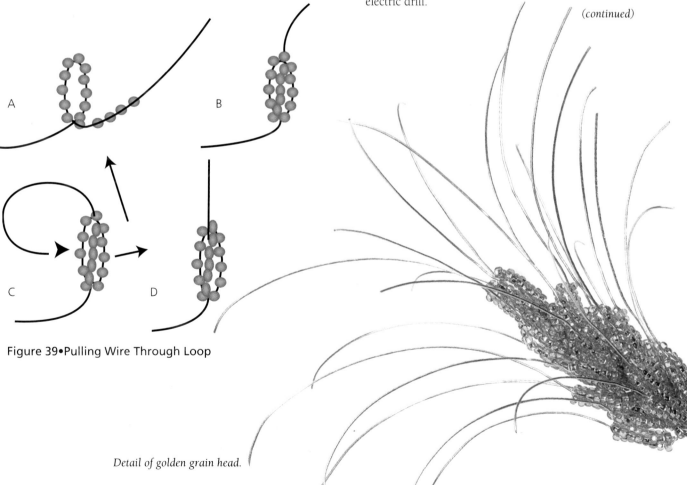

Figure 39•Pulling Wire Through Loop

Detail of golden grain head.

ASSEMBLY

1·Set aside five seeds for the bottom row.

2·Matching the bottom of the loops to the top of the stem, use 30-gauge wire to secure two seeds to the tip of the stem.

3·Drop down ¼" and secure two more.

4·Leaving ¼" between rows, add four rows of three seeds each, and then add a row of four seeds.

5·Use the reserved five seeds for the last row. However, when securing this row, keep your 30-gauge assembly wire very close to the beads. Do not cut it from the spool.

6·Pull the bottom row of seeds down so that they are pointing toward the bottom of the stem.

7·Using needle nose pliers, grab each wire that is extending down the stem and pull them very tightly upward, between the seeds of the last row.

8·Use the pliers to pinch these wires firmly against the stem.

9·Bring the assembly wire up and use several firm wraps to secure these bent wires. Finish by wrapping several times around one of the seed stems of the next-to-the-last four-seed row, as shown (Figure 40).

10·Trim all of these wires even with the base of the beads of the four-seed row.

11·Pull the bottom row back into position. Arch the top wires and cut to attractive lengths.

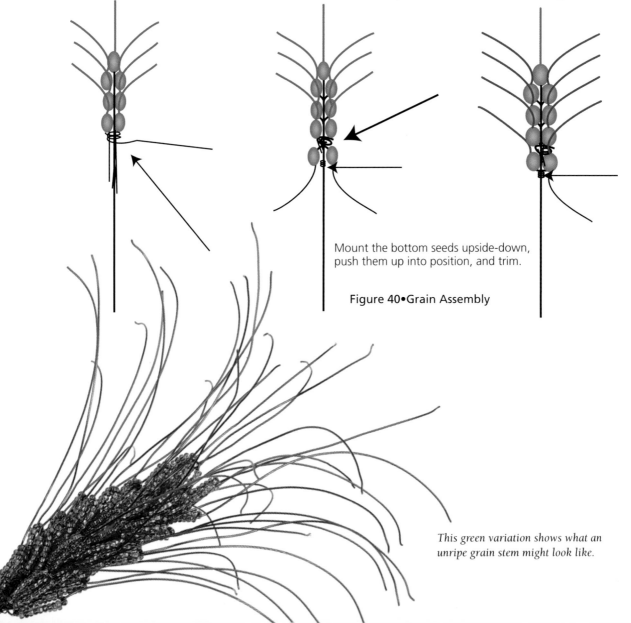

Mount the bottom seeds upside-down, push them up into position, and trim.

Figure 40•Grain Assembly

This green variation shows what an unripe grain stem might look like.

Ghost Orchid

After reading a book about orchids, I became obsessed with trying to find a picture of this flower. Finally, after contacting numerous orchid growers, I found a picture and complete dimensions. Most people will never see a live specimen, but with this pattern, you can have a beaded one grace your home as a wall plaque.

ghost orchid

Materials

- ½-hank white 10/0 or 11/0 seed beads
- 4 red seed beads
- 4 yellow seed beads
- 26-gauge white or silver beading wire
- 30-gauge white or silver assembly wire
- 6 18"-long 16-gauge paper-covered stem wires
- ½" light green floral tape
- Wooden log or slab
- Large staple

Petals (white)

Make 3 (pointed top, round bottom): 1" basic, five rows.
- **1•** Add two beads to the basic wire after row 3 on each.
- **2•** Reduce to two wires.

Make 2 (pointed top, round bottom): 1¼" basic, five rows.
- **1•** Add two beads to the basic wire after row 3 on each.
- **2•** Reduce to two wires.

Make 1 (round top, round bottom): one-bead basic, nine rows.
- **1•** After row 3, bend the top basic wire backwards about 45 degrees. As you continue beading, you will be forming a cup shape.
- **2•** After row 5, measure 6" of bare wire and cut the petal from the spool.
- **3•** As you add beads to the cut wire to complete rows 6 through 9, position a red bead, two yellow beads, and another red bead so that when you wrap around the top basic wire, there is one red and one yellow bead on either side of the top basic wire, as shown (Figure 41).
- **4•** Reduce to two wires.

Figure 41• Colored Bead Placement, Viewed From Tip of Petal

Stamen and Nectar Tube (white)

Make 1 (twisted loop) as follows:
- **1•** Leave 3" of bare wire, use 2" of beads to form a loop.
- **2•** Twist the wires and then twist the loop of beads into a spiral.
- **3•** Use 10" of beads to form another loop in the same manner.
- **4•** End with 3" of bare wire, cut from the spool, and twist wires (Figure 42).

Make 2 (pointed top, round bottom): 1" basic, seven rows.
- **1•** Begin with a top basic wire of at least 7" (only 1" of beads).
- **2•** After row 3, add two beads to the top basic wire.
- **3•** After row 5, add 4" of beads to the top basic wire.
- **4•** After completing the last two rows, use 2½" of beads to form a loop by the stem. Pinch the loop closed and position it along the side of the petal. Place one loop on the right side of one of the petals and the other on the left side of the other.
- **5•** Reduce to two wires.
- **6•** Lace the two petals together and in place where shown (Figure 43).
- **7•** Twist the stem wires together.

Figure 42•Stamen and Nectar Tube

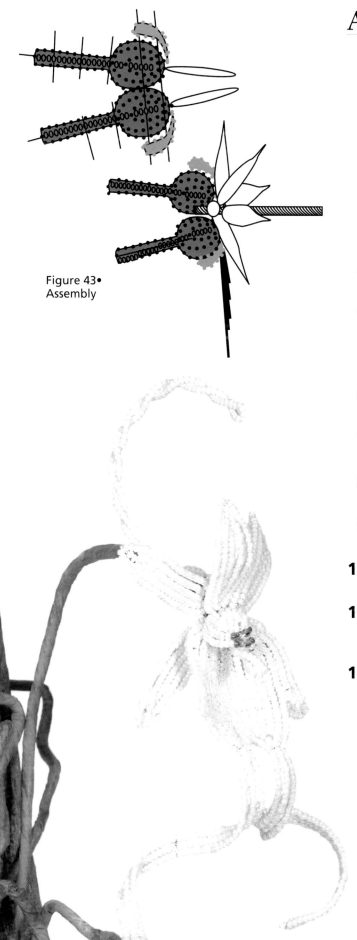

**Figure 43•
Assembly**

Close-up of ghost orchid.

ASSEMBLY

1• Use floral tape to cover all of the stem wires. If you are not able to get paper-covered stem wires, cut $1/2$" strips of brown paper, brush the backs with diluted white glue, and then wrap the stems as you would with floral tape. Let dry overnight before wrapping them with floral tape.

2• Lay the stamen (short end) along the center of the large "combined" petal, with their wires together. Position the cup shaped petal, opening downward, over the stamen. Secure them together with several wraps of assembly wire.

3• Add the two larger petals, followed by the three smaller petals, and secure these also.

4• Taper all of the wires to different lengths.

5• Use assembly wire to tightly attach the flower to the end of one of the stem wires. Wrap assembly area with floral tape.

6• Halfway down the stem, kink the stem wire every $1/2$" to $3/4$".

7• Put kinks along the entire length of all of the remaining stem wires.

8• Gather all of the stems together (including the flower), staggering them so the ends are not even.

9• Use wire to tie the center into a tight bundle and cover the wire with floral tape.

10• Position the flower in the approximate center of your log. Secure in place with a large wood staple.

11• Bend and wrinkle all of the wires to form a tangled bundle of roots. Try to push most of the tips into crevasses or around the back of the log.

12• Arc the flower stem up and back down. Slightly cup the combined petal. Pull the long tips apart outward and curl back down and inward.

Carnation

Materials

- 1½ hanks red 11/0 seed beads
- ½-hank green 11/0 seed beads
- 24-gauge colored beading wire
- 24-gauge green paddle wire
- 30-gauge assembly wire
- 18"-long 16-gauge stem wire
- ½" green floral tape

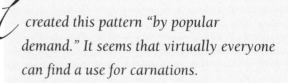

I created this pattern "by popular demand." It seems that virtually everyone can find a use for carnations.

Petals (continuous loops)

Make 3 (red) as follows:

1•Leave 2" of bare wire.
2•Using 1" of beads per loop, make five continuous loops.
3•End with 1" of bare wire, cut from the spool, bring wires together, and twist.

Make 4 (red) as follows:

1•Leave 2" of bare wire.
2•Using 1½" of beads per loop, make five continuous loops.
3•End with 1" of bare wire and cut from the spool. Do not twist ends together.
4•Pinch loops closed, shape into a petal, and lace.

Make 5 (red) as follows:

1•Leave 2" of bare wire.
2•Using 2" of beads per loop, make eight continuous loops.
3•End with 1" of bare wire and cut from the spool. Do not twist ends together.
4•Finish the same as the small petals.

Make 6 (red) as follows:

1•Leave 2" of bare wire.
2•Using 2½" of beads per loop, make eight continuous loops.
3•End with 1" of bare wire and cut from the spool. Do not twist ends together.
4•Finish the same as the small petals.

Sepals (continuous loops)

Make 1 (green) as follows:

1•Leave 2" of bare wire.
2•Alternate continuous loops of 3" and 2" of beads until you have 10 loops, five of each size.
3•End with 2" of bare wire and cut from spool. Do not twist ends together.
4•Leaving a tail of wire at each end, lace across the loops at a level even with the top of the small loops.
5•Connect the two sides together by twisting the two tails of lacing wire.
6•Twist the bottom wires to complete the sepal tube.

Bud (continuous loops)

Make 1 (red) as follows:

1•Leave 6" of bare wire.
2•Using 1½" of beads per loop, make eight continuous loops.
3•End with 6" of bare wire, cut from the spool, bring wires together, and twist.

Bud Sepal (continuous loops)

Make 1 (green) as follows:

1•Leave 6" of bare wire.
2•Alternate continuous loops of 2" and 1½" of beads until you have 10 loops, five of each size.
3•End with 6" of bare wire and cut from spool. Do not twist ends together.
4•Leaving a tail of wire at each end, lace across the loops at a level even with the top of the small loops.
5•Connect the two sides together by twisting the two tails of lacing wire.
6•Twist the bottom wires to complete the sepal tube.

Leaves (loops)

Make 2 (green) as follows:

1•Leave 1" of bare wire.
2•Make one loop, using 3" of beads.
3•End with 1" of bare wire, cut from the spool, bring ends together, and twist.

Make 2 (green) as follows:

1•Leave 1" of bare wire.
2•Make one four-row crossover loop, using 5" of beads for the first loop
3•End with 1" of bare wire, cut from the spool, bring ends together, and twist.

(continued)

ASSEMBLY

1. Lightly tape the stem wire.

2. Slip the red bud inside the bud sepal.

3. Fold two 12" pieces of 24-gauge wire in half and slip them down through the bud and sepal.

4. Twist the wires together and wrap floral tape around the top 3". Set aside.

5. Use assembly wire to attach the small loops to the top of the stem wire.

6. Keeping the assembly wire close and tight, add the petals one at a time, smallest to largest.

7. Feather the remaining lengths of wire, secure, and cover with floral tape.

8. Slip the sepal tube into position, as tight as possible, against the bottom of the flower.

9. Secure with assembly wire.

10. Drop down the stem about $3\frac{1}{2}$", position the bud and the two small leaves, and secure with assembly wire.

11. Position the two large leaves several inches down the stem and secure with assembly wire.

12. Use floral tape to wrap the entire stem, curl the leaves, and "wrinkle" the petals.

By using continuous loops of beads in varying lengths, you are able to achieve the look of the wavy edges a real carnation's petals have.

Lilac

*T*he extra time it takes to make
this flower is well worth the effort.
Everyone who sees it will "ooh" in
delight. Even though it is rather time-
consuming, you are going to want a
whole bouquet. Choose white, pink,
lavender, or purple for a lush and
lovely arrangement.

Materials

* 1⅔ hanks petal-colored 11/0 seed beads
* ¾ hank green 11/0 seed beads
* 70 yellow beads
* 28-gauge gold beading wire
* 26-gauge green beading or floral paddle wire
* 30-gauge green paddle wire (lacing and assembly)
* 18"-long 16-gauge stem wire
* Green floral tape
* Brown floral tape

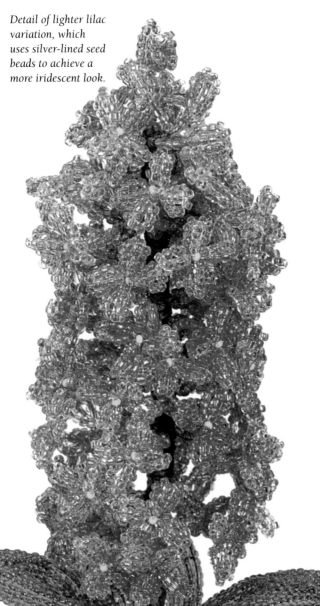

*Detail of lighter lilac
variation, which
uses silver-lined seed
beads to achieve a
more iridescent look.*

Buds (crossover loops)
Make 6 (petal color) as follows:
1 • Leave 2" of bare wire.
2 • Using nine beads for the first loop, make one four-row
crossover loop.
3 • End with 2" of bare wire, cut from the spool, bring
ends together, and twist the two wires smoothly.
4 • Place four petal-colored beads on the twisted wire,
followed by two green beads.
5 • For ease in handling, twist the buds together in pairs
(three pairs total).

Short Flowers (crossover loops)
Make 12 (petal color) as follows:
1 • Leave 2" of bare wire.
2 • Using nine beads for the first loop, make four three-
row crossover loops.
3 • Pull a bare section of the beaded wire across the top,
center of the flower, and continue down the other
side.
4 • End with 2" bare wire and cut from spool. Do not
twist ends together.
5 • Pull the other cut wire across the top of the flower,
perpendicular to the first. Place one yellow bead on
the wire, center the bead in the middle of the flower,
and pull the wire back down to the bottom.
6 • Place six petal-colored and two green beads on each
wire.
7 • Twist the wires smoothly and add two green beads to
the twisted wire.
8 • For ease in handling, twist the finished flowers
together in pairs (six pairs total).

Long Flowers (crossover loops)
Make 64 (petal color) as follows:
1. Leave 2" of bare wire.
2. Using nine beads for the first loop, make four three-row crossover loops.
3. Pull a bare section of the beaded wire across the top, center of the flower, and continue down the other side.
4. End with 2" bare wire and cut from spool. Do not twist ends together.
5. Pull the other cut wire across the top of the flower, perpendicular to the first. Place one yellow bead on the wire, center the bead in the middle of the flower, and pull the wire back down to the bottom.
6. Place eight petal-colored and three green beads on each wire.
7. Twist the wires smoothly and add two green beads to the twisted wire.
8. For ease in handling, twist the finished flowers together in pairs (32 total pairs).

Leaves (pointed top, round bottom)
Make 2 (green): 1/4" basic, 17 rows.
1. To form a better point, add an extra bead to the basic wire between the rows.
2. Leave three wires and twist.
3. Tape with green floral tape and lace.

Make 2 (green): 1/4" basic, 21 rows.
1. To form a better point, add an extra bead to the basic wire between the rows.
2. Leave three wires and twist.
3. Tape with green floral tape and lace.

ASSEMBLY

1. Using brown floral tape, lightly tape the stem wire.
2. Secure the assembly wire to the top of the stem.
3. As you spiral the wire down the stem, secure the buds at the top, the short flowers in the center, and the long flowers at the bottom. It may take three to four pairs to go completely around the stem. Make sure, as you move down the stem, the next row of flowers is no more than 3/8" below the previous row.
4. When all of the flowers are secure, cut a piece of brown floral tape in half lengthwise and tape over all of the visible wires.
5. Beginning 1" below the flower head, use assembly wire to secure the two small leaves directly across from each other.
6. Secure the large pair of leaves 1" further down.
7. Tape the entire stem with brown floral tape.

Close-up of lilac variation made with darker beads.

Floribunda Rose

Materials

* 2¼ hanks petal-colored 11/0 seed beads
* 1 hank green 11/0 seed beads
* 26-gauge colored beading wire
* 26-gauge green beading or paddle wire
* 30-gauge wire (lacing and assembly)
* ½" green floral tape
* 3 18"-long 16-gauge stem wires

After creating the sweetheart rose for my first book, I realized that I needed something larger and softer. Not only does this fit the bill, but any one of the three parts can be used alone. One large, full bloom, a small rose, and a bud are all together in one lovely group.

floribunda rose

Large Flower (round top, round bottom)

Make 2 (petal color): one-bead basic, 11 rows.
Reduce each to one wire and twist.

Make 3 (petal color): one-bead basic, 15 rows.
1•Reduce to one wire and twist.
2•Lace all of the petals.

Make 4 (petal color): one-bead basic, 19 rows.
1•Reduce to one wire and twist.
2•Lace all of the petals.

Make 5 (petal color): one-bead basic, 23 rows.
1•Reduce to one wire and twist.
2•Lace all of the petals.

Small Flower (round top, round bottom)

Make 2 (petal color): one-bead basic, 11 rows.
Reduce to one wire and twist.

Make 3 (petal color): one-bead basic, 15 rows.
1•Reduce to one wire and twist.
2•Lace all of the petals.

Make 4 (petal color): one-bead basic, 19 rows.
1•Reduce to one wire and twist.
2•Lace all of the petals.

Bud (round top, round bottom)

Make 2 (petal color): one-bead basic, 11 rows.
Reduce each to one wire and twist.

Make 3 (petal color): one-bead basic, 15 rows.
1•Reduce each to one wire and twist.
2•Lace all of the petals.

Sepals (pointed top, round bottom)

Make 12 (green): eight-bead basic, nine rows.
1•To form an elongated point, add two beads to the basic wire after rows 3, 5, and 7.
2•Reduce to one wire and twist.

Leaves (pointed top, round bottom)

Make 2 (green): eight-bead basic, 11 rows.
Leave three wires and twist.

Make 4 (green): eight-bead basic, seven rows.
Leave three wires and twist.

(continued)

Detail of yellow flower, which is assembled with 14 petals in four sizes.

ASSEMBLY

1. Lightly tape your stem wires.

2. For each of the three flowers, start by folding the two smallest petals in half lengthwise toward the "wrong side."

3. With the folds overlapping, hold the two small petals so that the bases are even with the top of the stem wire.

4. Using assembly wire, tightly wrap the petals in place with two to three passes.

5. One at a time, position each of the next largest petals around the stem and secure in the same manner. When all are added, go on to the next size and repeat the procedure.

TIP: In steps 4 and 5, make sure to place each row tightly against the previous row. Failure to do so will leave unsightly gaps in your bloom.

6. When all of the petals have been added, arrange the sepals in the same manner: five for the large flower, four for the small flower, and three for the bud. Secure and cut the assembly wire.

7. Turn the roses upside-down, pull the wires slightly away from the stem, and cut them to all different lengths. This will form a tapered effect when they are pressed back against the stem.

8. Secure the wires and tape each of the stems again.

9. Group the three blooms together and secure them with assembly wire.

10. Wire the leaf groups (below) to the stem and cover all of the assembly areas with floral tape.

Leaf Group Assembly

1. After twisting the wires, cut a length of floral tape in half lengthwise.

2. Beginning at the base of the beads, tape about halfway down each leaf.

3. With the largest leaf at the top and the two small ones opposite each other as shown (Figure 44), hold the leaves and twist the wires together.

4. Tape the twisted area and flatten the lower half slightly. (This will lessen any bulges on the flower stem.)

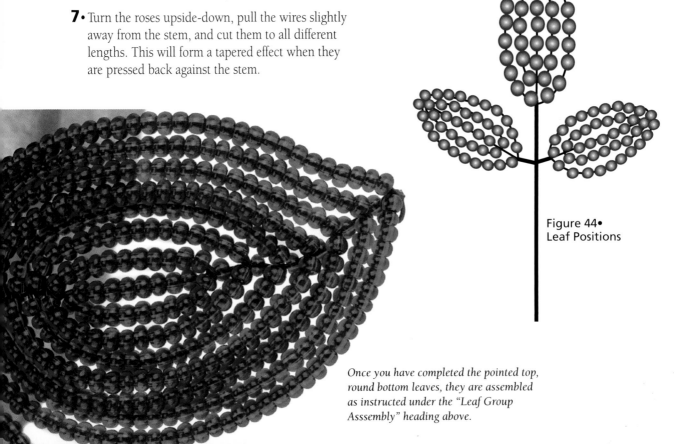

Figure 44•
Leaf Positions

Once you have completed the pointed top, round bottom leaves, they are assembled as instructed under the "Leaf Group Asssembly" heading above.

Columbine

My husband is a big fan of the red and yellow combination. So, this flower was created according to his specs. Not only is this delicate flower fun to make, the possible color combinations are nearly endless. What a great way to use up small amounts of leftover beads!

columbine

Materials

- 6 strands inner color 11/0 seed beads
- 7 strands outer color 11/0 seed beads
- 15 matte yellow 11/0 seed beads
- 2 strands green 11/0 seed beads
- 30-gauge gold wire (stamens, spurs, and assembly)
- 24- or 26-gauge colored beading wire
- 18"-long 16-gauge stem wire
- ½" green floral tape

Inner Petals (round top, round bottom)
Make 5 (inner color): 1" basic, nine rows.
1. Reduce to one wire and twist.
2. Approximately ⅜" from the bottom, lace across the front of each petal.
3. Fold the petal inward, side to side, and tack the two sides together at the lacing.
4. Flare the tops of the petals out and back.

Outer Petals (pointed top, round bottom)
Make 5 (outer color): 1" basic, nine rows.
Reduce each to one wire and twist.

Spurs
Make 5 (outer color) as follows:
1. Cut 6" of 30-gauge wire.
2. Hold the wire in half to mark the center.
3. Place 1" of beads on the wire, positioned so that the end of the row is at the center mark.
4. Thread the other end of the wire back through all of the beads, except the one closest to the center (Figure 45).

Although my color choice was red and yellow, another popular columbine color combination is white for the inner petals and a periwinkle for the outer petals.

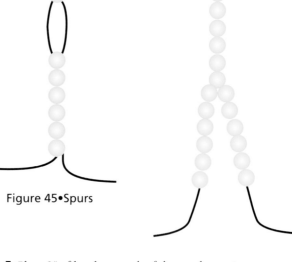

Figure 45•Spurs

5. Place 1" of beads on each of the two bare wires.
6. Twist the bare end wires together for their entire length.

Stamens

Make 1 (matte yellow on gold wire) as follows:

1•Put the yellow beads on the gold 30-gauge wire.
2•Position one bead 3" from the end of the wire, as shown (Figure 46-A).
3•Hold the bead and twist the wire for 1" (Figure 46-B).
4•Position the next bead 1" from the first and twist.
5•Continue in this manner (Figure 46-C) until you have 15 stamens.
6•End with 2" of bare wire and cut from the spool.
7•Bring the bottom wires together and twist.

Leaflets (loops)

Make 3 (green) as follows:

1•Leave 4" of bare wire.
2• Leaving a very small space between loops, make a single loop with 1" of beads, a single loop with 1½" of beads, a two-row loop with 1½" of beads for the first (inner) loop, a single loop with 1½" of beads, and a single loop with 1" of beads, as shown (Figure 47).
3•End with 4" of bare wire and cut from spool.
4•Pinch the loops closed, push them together, and lace.
5•Put two beads on each of the end wires, bring the ends together directly under the center loop, and twist the wires together.
6•Tape the top half of the stems with floral tape.
7•Stack the three leaflets and twist their stems together about ½" from the beads.
8•Re-tape the stem.

ASSEMBLY

1• Lightly tape the stem wire.

2• Using assembly wire, attach the stamen group to the end of the stem. Make sure that the bottoms of the stamens are even with the top of the stem wire.

3• Match the bottom beads of a spur to the bottom beads on the back of an outer petal. Wind the spur wire around and down the petal stem securely. Repeat with the remaining spurs and petals.

4• Attach all five inner petals directly below the stamen group.

5• Attach the outer petals just below and between the inner petals.

6• Wind the assembly wire about 4" down the stem wire.

7• Secure the leaflet group in place.

8• Tape the entire stem wire.

9• Shape the spurs in a gentle outward arc.

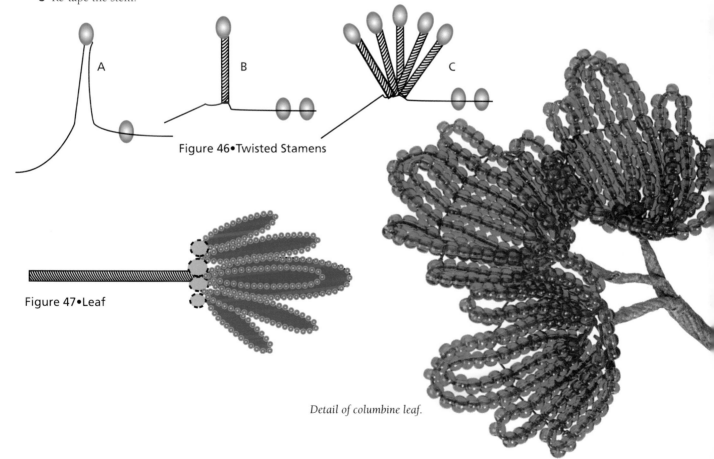

Figure 46•Twisted Stamens

Figure 47•Leaf

Detail of columbine leaf.

Freesia

Materials

- 1 hank petal-colored 11/0 seed beads
- ¼ strand green 11/0 seed beads
- 18 yellow 11/0 seed beads
- 24- or 26-gauge beading wire
- 28- or 30-gauge lacing/assembly wire (match wire to bead color as
- closely as possible)
- 18"-long 16-gauge stem wire
- ½" green floral tape

Every time I see a bouquet, it contains freesia. How could I ignore the unique shape when creating bouquets of my own? Since it is usually used as a filler, be creative when choosing your colors.

freesia

Petals (round top, round bottom)

Make 18 (petal color): 10-bead basic, seven rows.

1•Begin row 1 and 2 as usual.

2•After completing row 2, wrap the beaded wire another half-turn around the top basic. Allow this wrap to go ¼" upward on the basic wire.

3•Add eight beads to the top of the basic wire.

4•Ignore the bottom half of the petal and complete six rows on the top portion only.

5•On row 7, bring the beads down to the break, crease it with your fingernail, and proceed all the way to the bottom to finish, as shown (Figure 48).

6•Reduce to one wire and twist.

Buds (round top, round bottom)

Make 1 (petal color): 16-bead basic, nine rows.
Make 1 (petal color): 12-bead basic, seven rows.
Make 1 (petal color): eight-bead basic, five rows.
Make 1 (green): seven-bead basic, five rows.

1•Leave three wires on each of the buds and twist.

2•Twist the entire petal into a spiral.

3•Use ¼" floral tape (½" tape cut in half lengthwise) to tape down approximately 1" of each stem.

Stamens
(continuous twisted loops on lacing wire)

Make 3 (yellow) as follows:

1•Leave 3" of bare wire.

2•Position a single bead and twist the wire for ½".

3•Position the next bead ½" from the first stamen and twist, as in Figure 46 of the Columbine instructions, page 75.

4•Continue in this manner until you have six stamens.

5•End with 2½" of bare wire, cut from the spool, and twist end wires together.

(continued)

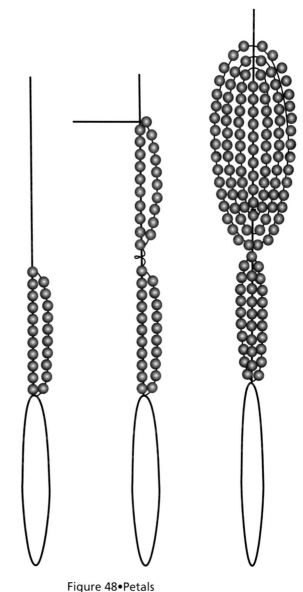

Figure 48•Petals

ASSEMBLY

1• Lightly tape the stem wire.

2• Cut 5" to 6" of lacing wire.

3• Leave a 1" tail of wire and secure the lacing wire in the "break" of the first petal. Working on the reverse sides and in one continuous action, lace across the "breaks" of a total of six petals. Since the tops are larger than the bottoms, overlap the tops, one to the front, one to the back, one to the front, and so on, as shown (Figure 49). Make sure that the edges of the lower portions are laced tightly together. Do not cut the lacing wire.

4• Bring the two ends of the lacing wire together, reverse sides of the petals facing outward, tightly twist them together, and trim to $^1/4$". Tuck the end between petals.

5• Push a pen or pencil down through the center of the group until the pointed end is even with the bottom of the petals. Use this to flatten and shape the lower portion of the flower into a tube.

6• With the pencil still in place, twist the wires for $^1/2$".

7• Drop a stamen group down through the top. Pull the twisted wire down through the bottom. Wrap it around and down the flower stem several times.

8• Taper the bulk of the stem by cutting the remaining wires to different lengths.

9• Use $^1/4$" floral tape to tape down 1" of the stem.

10• Allow the three inner petals to remain slightly upright. Flare the three outer petals downward.

11• Complete the remaining two flowers in the same manner.

12• Bend each of the flower and bud stems 90 degrees: small buds $^1/4$" from the beads; medium buds $^3/8$" from the beads; and the flower stems $^1/2$" from the beads.

13• Use a continuous length of assembly wire to attach the buds (smallest to largest) and flowers to the stem. Place the green bud at the tip and allow approximately $^1/2$" between buds. Between the large bud and the first flower (and between flowers) allow at least 1" of stem.

14• Cover all assembly areas with floral tape. It is easier to tape between the flowers if you use $^1/4$" tape.

15• Tape the lower stem.

Detail of freesia petals.

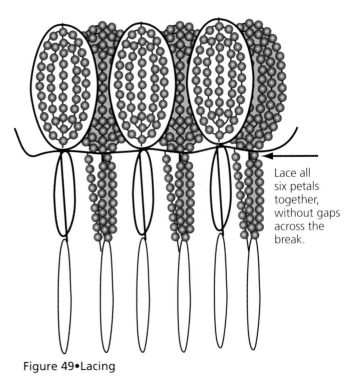

Lace all six petals together, without gaps across the break.

Figure 49•Lacing

Passion Flower and Fruit

Jhis unusual tropical plant is a sunburst of color and shapes. It's fun to make and fun to view. The flower itself has been given a history of religious significance, and the fruit can be either yellow or purple.

passion flower and fruit

Materials

- 1 hank white 11/0 seed beads
- 2 strands dark purple 11/0 seed beads
- 2 strands light purple 11/0 seed beads
- 2 strands light green 11/0 seed beads
- 1 strand red 11/0 seed beads
- 1¼ hanks dark green 11/0 seed beads
- ¾-hank yellow or purple 11/0 seed beads (fruit)
- 28-gauge gold wire (fruit)
- 24- or 26-gauge colored beading wire
- 24- or 26-gauge green beading or paddle wire
- 30-gauge wire (lacing and assembly)
- 18"-long 16-gauge stem wire
- ½" green floral tape
- Plastic, wood, or polystyrene egg (choose a color or paint the egg to match the beads)
- Glue

Petals (slightly pointed top, round bottom)

Make 10 (white): 1" basic, nine rows.

Reduce each to one wire and twist.

Stamens

Make 50 (purple and white) as follows:

1• Thread 10 dark purple, six white, and eight light purple beads onto the 28-gauge wire.
2• Skipping the light purple bead closest to the end, thread the wire back through the row of beads.
3• Cut the two bare wires to 1".
4• When you have completed five stamens, twist their wires together.
5• Matching the bases, put the stamen group on the surface of a petal.
6• Wrap the stamen wires tightly around the petal's stem wire.
7• Do this to all the petals.

Center Disk (round)

Make 1 (dark purple and light green) as follows:

1• Cut 3 feet beading wire. Without beads, form the basic wire and loop.
2• Do not put any beads on the basic wire (row 1).
3• Use three dark purple beads for each of rows 2 and 3. Bow these rows slightly so that there is a hole in the center of the disk.
4• Use dark purple beads for rows 4 through 7.
5• Use light green beads for rows 8 through 13.
6• Use dark purple beads for rows 14 and 15.
7• Do not cut the top basic wire.
8• Reduce to one wire and twist.
9• Bring the top and bottom wires together in the center of the back and twist.

Center Star (continuous loops)

Make 1 (light green) as follows:

1• Crimp the end of the wire so the beads cannot slide off the end.
2• Leave 12 beads on 2" of bare wire and make two nine-bead continuous loops.
3• Leave 24 beads and make two more nine-bead continuous loops.
4• Continue in the same manner until you have made five sets of continuous loops, each separated by 24 beads.
5• End with 12 beads and 2" of bare wire, cut from the spool, and twist the bare ends together.
6• Hold one of the pairs of loops, closest to the twisted wires.
7• Twist the loops until the 12 beads on the end are twisted with the first 12 beads of the 24-bead group.
8• Repeat step 7 for all of the loops so you have five spokes and then arrange the loops so that they form a "T" with the twisted wires, as shown (Figure 50).

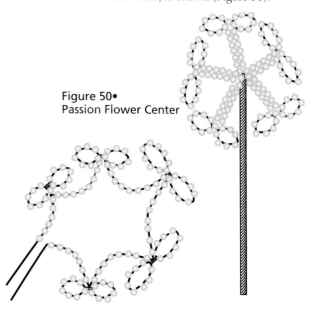

Figure 50•
Passion Flower Center

Pistils (continuous loops)

Make 1 (red) as follows:

1•Using the same technique as in the center star, begin with 16 beads.

2•Make three nine-bead continuous loops.

3•Leave 32 beads and form the next group of loops.

4•Continue until you have three groups of loops.

5•Finish and twist in the same manner as the center star.

6•Fold the loops down against the twisted spokes to form "knobs" on the ends of the three pistils.

Tendrils

Make 4 (light green) as follows:

1•Cut four 6" pieces of 24-gauge wire.

2•Put 4" of beads on each wire and crimp both ends so the beads cannot slide off.

Leaves (pointed top, pointed bottom)

Make 6 (dark green): $1\frac{1}{2}$" basic, seven rows.

Reduce each to one wire and twist.

Make 6 (dark green): 2" basic, nine rows.

1•Reduce each to one wire and twist.

2•Lace each leaf once across the center.

Make 3 (dark green): $2\frac{1}{2}$" basic, 11 rows.

1•Reduce each to one wire and twist.

2•Lace each leaf once across the center.

Fruit

Make 1 (bright yellow or dark purple) as follows:

If you are using a plastic egg, use Superglue. If you are using a polystyrene or wood egg, use white craft glue.

You may either leave the beads on the original strings or transfer them onto 30-gauge wire. If you leave them on the original string, simply tie the ends of the strings together when adding more beads.

1•Beginning at the center bottom, apply the glue to the egg in no more than a $\frac{1}{2}$" band at a time.

2•Spiral the beads around the egg.

3•Allow one section to dry before proceeding.

ASSEMBLY

1• Lightly tape the stem wire. Cut off a 3" piece to use for the flower.

2• Push the twisted wire of the pistils through the center of the center star.

3• Push both of the pistil and center star wires through the center hole in the center disk.

4• Twist all of the wires together.

5• Use assembly wire to attach the piece created in step 4 to the end of the 3" stem wire. Position it so that the stem wire just barely touches the back of the disk.

6• Position and secure around the stem five petals with attached stamens.

7• Once secure, attach the last five petals directly below the spaces between the first five petals.

8• Gently pull all of the stamens up, through the spaces, to form a solid ring around the center disk.

9• Tape over the assembly area.

10• To form the leaf groups, make a stack of two medium leaves, two small leaves, and one large leaf. Twist the wires together. Fan the leaves into order: small, medium, large, and medium small.

11• Tape the stems.

12• To the top of the long stem wire, use assembly wire to attach one leaf group (match the base of the group to the top of the stem), one tendril (slide all the beads to one end and secure tightly at the base of the beads), and the fruit (1" of taped stem left free for fruit to dangle).

13• Drop down 3" and attach the flower (leave 2" of flower stem) and one tendril.

14• Drop down 3" and secure a leaf group (leave 1" of free stem) and one tendril. Repeat.

15• Tape the entire stem. Bend and shape the stem and leaves to form a vine.

16• Wrap the tendrils around a pencil to shape spirals.

Note the detail you achieve when bringing all six different flower components together.

Lily of
the Valley

Materials

- 2 strands white 11/0 seed beads
- 2 hanks medium green 11/0 seed beads
- 24- or 26-gauge white beading wire
- 26-gauge green beading or paddle wire
- 4 6"-long pieces 22-gauge green wire (to stiffen leaves)
- ½" green floral tape

Flowers (continuous loops)

Make 1 (white) as follows:

1•Leave 4" of bare wire.
2•Make five continuous loops, using ½" of beads for each loop.
3•Bring the wire across the top of the flower and down the other side.
4•Below the flower, twist the two bottom wires together for ½".
5•Leave 1¼" of bare wire and make another flower in the same manner as steps 2 through 4.
6•Continue until you have eight flowers.
7•Leave 1" of wire and make four continuous loops.
8•Pinch all of the loops closed.
9•In the middle of each loop, place a sharp upward bend.
10•Pull the loops toward the centers and form each flower into a little cup.
11•Measure enough wire to go back to the cut end.
12•Hold onto the top flower and twist the entire length (Figure 51).
13•If your wire is too flexible to stand upright, twist another piece down the entire length of the stem.
14•Cut about 8" of floral tape in half lengthwise.
15•Beginning at a point halfway between the top two flowers, tape down the entire stem.
16•Bend a slight arch in each of the little flower stems.

Make 1 (white):

Make like the first, except forming only five flowers before the smaller flower at the tip.

Leaves (pointed top, pointed bottom)

Make 4 (green): 2¼" basic, 27 rows.

1•Lace all leaves.
2• Use 6" of 22-gauge wire to stiffen the stems as in Stem Stiffening Option 2, page 16.

A lthough this flower is most recognized for its scent, the beaded variety is an eye-catching way to add greenery to your arrangements. A simple flower deserves a simple pattern. I hope you agree that this one serves that purpose.

lily of the valley

ASSEMBLY

1• Gather all of the stems together and wire in place tightly.
2• Trim bottom wire to approximately 2".
3• Use floral tape to cover the stem.

*Detail of lily of the valley,
a simple, yet elegant, pattern.*

Twist the entire length.

Figure 51•Flower Twisting

Bee

*W*hat can I say? One afternoon with the grandkids, and they had me gluing eyes on everything! This little bee is attached to a pin finding to create a fun stickpin, but it could be displayed on its own or as an embellishment to any number of home decorating projects.

bee

Materials

- Less than 1 strand yellow 10/0 or 11/0 seed beads
- Less than 1 strand black 10/0 or 11/0 seed beads
- 1 strand clear (or white) 10/0 or 11/0 seed beads
- 26-gauge goldtone wire
- Super glue
- E6000 glue (optional)
- Pin finding (optional)
- Black gloss paint (optional)

Bee Wings (round top, round bottom)
Make 4 (clear): $1/2$" basic, five rows.

1. Do not twist wires.
2. Decide whether your bee should have just legs, just antennae, or both legs and antennae. If you want both, cut a 6" piece of wire for the antennae and fold it in half. (This can also be two 6" pieces twisted together and then folded in half.)

ASSEMBLY

1. Lightly tape the top 3" of the stem wire.

2. On all of the wing pieces, spread the basic wires apart so they are easy to identify.

3. With "wrong" sides facing up, lay two of the wings on top of each other.

4. Match the bases of the wings and twist only the center wires together.

5. Repeat with the other set.

6. Spread the wings open slightly.

7. Hold the two sections together with the wrong sides facing outward. You are now displaying 10 wires; two are twisted, eight are not.

8. Choosing one untwisted wire from each side, twist them together, and continue, two at a time. You should now have six twisted wires (legs). Open the wings slightly.

Note: If you have chosen to have just legs, bend three of the wires to the right and three to the left.

If you have chosen to have just antennae, bend three of the wires sharply forward, and bend three wires sharply backward.

If you want both, space the legs as above. Thread the folded piece of wire behind the bee's front legs. Twist the $^1/_4$" of wire closest to the legs and position the antennae forward. At this stage, it is OK if the antennae are floppy.

9. Have two wires, one with yellow and one with black beads. Holding them together, use at least three wraps of the bare wires to position the wires at the very tip of the taped end. Tug on the wire to make sure it is secure.

10. Position the underside of the bee on the stem wire so that its center (point where all of the wings meet) is $^5/_8$" from the tip of the stem wire and the antennae are hanging off the end. If you are not making legs, three twisted wires should extend beyond the tip.

11. Wrap the body with both yellow and black at the same time by sliding the beads (on the wire) forward. After several wraps (about $^1/_2$"), pull the two front legs forward. Wrap once or twice and pull the second set of legs forward. Do the same to position the last set. When you arrive at the center point of the wings (probably between sets of legs) wrap one beaded wire over and between the wings. Pull the bead wrap very tight.

12. Continue wrapping until you have a 1" body length. Let the beads slide back and use three wraps tight against the beads to finish.

13. Bend and trim the legs and antennae. If you have no legs, trim off one of the three twisted wires at the tip.

14. Trim off any exposed floral tape or construction wires that extend beyond the tail.

15. On the tip and tail end of the body, very carefully place a very small drop of "super type" glue on the stem wire. Tilt the bug so that the glue runs under the first row of beads. Never put glue on the visible surface of the beads as it will dull the shine.

16. The bee is now ready to be used in a bouquet by bending the stem wire to the desired angle.

For a pin:

1. Cut the stem wire close to the tail.

2. Apply several small drops of clear craft glue (E600) to the back of a suitably sized pin finding. Position the pin along the belly and press gently.

3. Taking care to not touch the wet glue, use three 2" pieces of wire to secure. Thread one through each hole of the finding. Wrap them once around the body and twist the ends until the wire is tight and no longer visible.

4. Trim the ends and tuck them between the finding and the body. Set aside to dry.

If there is glue visible after drying, use manicure scissors and tweezers to remove the excess.

If the cut ends of the wire are noticeable, use a very fine brush to paint them black.

5. Glue on eyes, if desired.

As you can see in this close-up of the bee, it is a fun project to do with school-aged children.

Dragonfly

- Less than 1 strand blue (or other color) 10/0 or 11/0 seed beads
- 3 strands clear (or white) 10/0 or 11/0 seed beads
- 26-gauge blue wire (for body)
- 26-gauge goldtone wire (for legs and wings)
- Super glue
- E6000 glue (optional)
- Pin finding (optional)
- Black gloss paint (optional)

This creation also arose from the afternoon with the grandkids. Like the bee, it could be mounted to a pin finding or displayed standing on its own. With the popularity of dragonflies in home décor today, it is a simple piece that adds big impact to any room.

dragonfly

Dragonfly Wings (round top, round bottom)

Make 4 (clear): 2" basic, five rows.

1• Do not twist wires.

2• Decide whether your bug should have just legs, just antennae, or both legs and antennae. If you want both, cut a 6" piece of wire for the antennae and fold it in half. (This can also be two 6" pieces twisted together and then folded in half.)

ASSEMBLY

1• Repeat steps 1 through 10 of the bee instructions, pages 84 and 85.

2• Slide the beads on the wire forward and begin beading the body. After several wraps (about ¹/2"), pull the two front legs forward. Wrap once or twice and pull the second set of legs forward. Do the same to position the last set. When you arrive at the center point of the wings (probably between sets of legs), wrap one beaded wire over and between the wings. Pull the bead wrap very tight.

3• Continue wrapping until you have 2¹/2". Let the beads slide back and use three wraps tight against the beads to finish.

4• Bend and trim the legs and antennae. If you have no legs, trim off one of the three twisted wires at the tip.

5• Trim off any exposed floral tape or construction wires that extend beyond the tail.

6• On the tip and tail end of the body, very carefully place a very small drop of "super type" glue on the stem wire. Tilt the bug so that the glue runs under the first row of beads. Never put glue on the visible surface of the beads as it will dull the shine.

7• The dragonfly is now ready to be used in a bouquet, simply by bending the stem wire to the desired angle. For a pin, refer to the instructions in the bee project, page 85.

Close-up of dragonfly, a cute little creature that is perfect for introducing a child to the art of French beading.

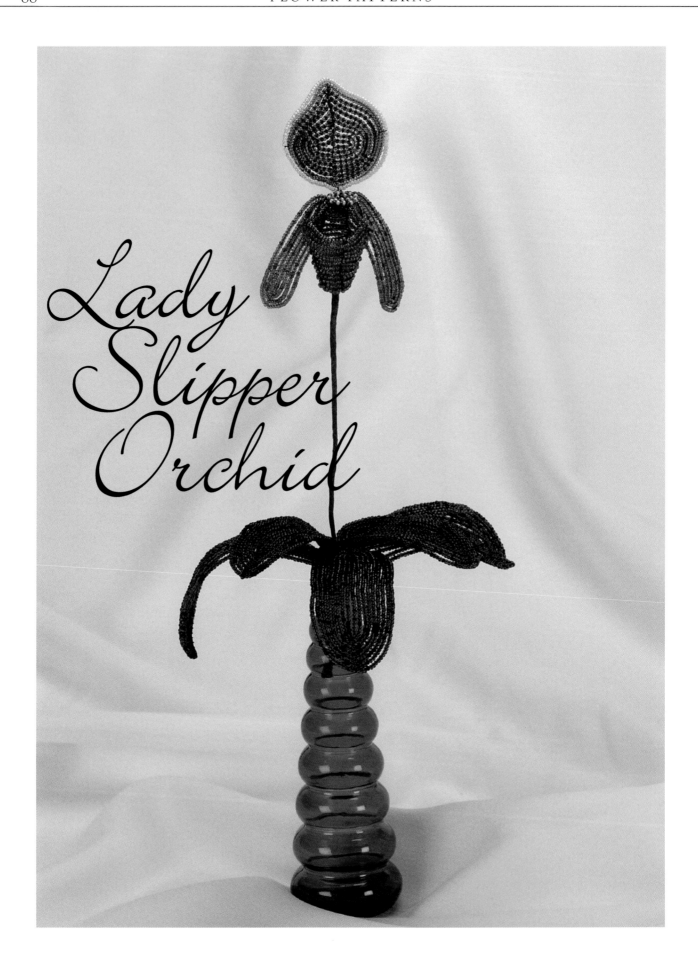

Lady Slipper Orchid

Materials

- 1 strand white 11/0 seed beads
- ½-hank light green 11/0 seed beads
- 1 hank medium green 11/0 seed beads
- ½-hank dark green 11/0 seed beads
- 4 strands maroon or purple 11/0 seed beads
- 24- or 26-gauge green beading or paddle wire
- 30-gauge assembly wire
- 18"-long 16-gauge stem wire
- 5 5"-long pieces of 22-gauge green wire (to stiffen leaves)
- ½" green floral tape
  *The bead amounts may vary, as the actual amounts used will depend on personal preference and style.

*W*hen this orchid first bloomed, I rejected it as a bead candidate. Then, the flower lasted for weeks and weeks, constantly taunting me. Finally, I gave in to the challenge.

lady slipper orchid

Petal #1 (round top, round bottom)
Make 1 (medium green and white): one-bead basic, five rows.

- **1•** Cut 12" of wire and then form a basic wire and loop.
- **2•** Use a green bead as the basic and then alternate the beads: one green, one white.
- **3•** Use seven beads for each of rows 2 and 3, pushing them down the basic wire to touch the one-bead basic.
- **4•** Complete rows 4 and 5.
- **5•** Leave three wires, cut from the spool, and twist.

Petals #2 and #3 (pointed top, round bottom)
Make 2 (light green and maroon): 2" basic, seven rows.

Randomly mix a small amount of maroon beads with the light green to produce speckles.

Petal #4 (pointed top, round bottom)
Make 1 (light green, medium green, and white): one-bead basic, 21 rows.

- **1•** Cut 3 feet of 26-gauge wire.
- **2•** Using one medium green bead as the basic row, form the basic loop and wire.
- **3•** Alternating light and medium green, use 12 beads for each of rows 2 and 3.
- **4•** Pinch the rows down to the basic bead, forcing the colors to line up. That is, light green over light green, medium green over medium green.
- **5•** Add a medium green bead to the basic now and each time you go around. Make sure to push the rows around the extra bead to close any gaps.
- **6•** As you continue, through the completion of row 17, use light and medium green beads to form the vertical stripes already started.
- **7•** Rows 18 and 19 should be completed in light green.
- **8•** Finish by making rows 20 and 21 white.
- **9•** Leave three wires, cut from the spool, and twist.
- **10•** Lace the petal across the center.

Cup (beehive)
Make 1 (maroon with random light green speckles): 15 "rounds."

- **1•** Cut two 6" pieces of 26-gauge wire.
- **2•** While matching the ends, hold the cut wires and the bare end of your beaded wire together.
- **3•** At the center, wrap the bare beaded wire twice around the bundle.
- **4•** Separate the wires to form five spokes with the beads attached in the center.
- **5•** Begin by placing one bead between the nearest two spokes and wrap the wire around the spoke, as if it were a "basic." Bend the cut end of this spoke to mark it as spoke 1.
- **6•** Complete round 1 by securing one bead in each space between spokes.
- **7•** Use the following list to complete the "cup." The number listed is the number of beads between spokes. When you have a "short spoke" followed by a "tall spoke," or visa versa, be sure to push the beads down to fill in the low spots.
  - Round 2: three beads
  - Rounds 3 and 4: four beads
  - Rounds 5 and 6: five beads
  - Rounds 7 and 8: six beads, add an extra bead to spoke wires 1, 2, 4, and 5.
  - Rounds 9 through 15: Continue adding an extra bead to spokes 1, 2, 4, and 5 each time around. Adjust the number of beads between the spokes to form an outward tapered beehive. The upper lip should be pointed at spokes 1, 2, 4, and 5. There should be dips between spokes 1 and 2 and spokes 4 and 5. Spoke 3 should be at the bottom of the largest dip.
- **8•** When complete, cut bead wire to 2" and twist it with spoke 1.

(continued)

ASSEMBLY

1· Lightly tape stem wire.

2· Using assembly wire, attach the "cup" to the end of the stem.

3· Position and attach petal #1 so that, when bent down, it covers the top of the "cup" wire.

4· Slightly bend the stem so that the "cup" hangs downward.

5· Position and attach petal #4 so that it points straight up.

6· Secure petals #2 and # 3 on either side, as shown (Figure 52).

7· Trim the wires to different lengths.

8· Wrap the assembly wire at least 8" down the stem.

9· Position the smallest leaf directly behind the stem and then alternate the larger leaves on either side.

10· Secure with the assembly wire.

11· Tape down the entire stem.

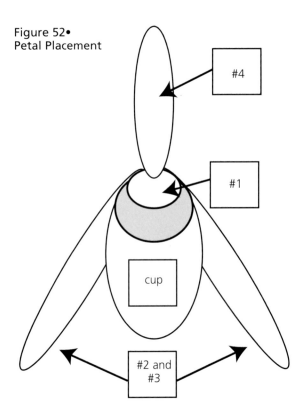

Figure 52•
Petal Placement

#4

#1

cup

#2 and #3

Detail of the lady slipper orchid's dainty petals and colorful cup.

Close-up of lady slipper leaf, which consists of a 3" basic, 17 rows made with two shades of green seed beads.

Miniatures

These little flowers can be used in miniature pots, jewelry items, or to decorate gifts and packages. They are also a great way to use up small quantities of beads left over from other projects.

miniatures

Materials

- Assorted colors of 10/0 or 11/0 seed beads (less than 1 strand per flower)
- 24- or 26-gauge wire
- ¼" floral tape (½" cut lengthwise)

Iris

Large Petals (round top, round bottom)
Make 3 (petal color): eight-bead basic, three rows.
1 • Use four yellow beads for the bottom of the basic row and four petal-colored beads at the top of the basic row.
2 • Reduce each to one wire.

Small Petals (continuous loops)
Make 1 (petal color) as follows:
1 • Leave 3" of bare wire.
2 • Make three 1" continuous loops.
3 • End with 3" of bare wire and cut from spool. Do not twist ends together.

ASSEMBLY

1 • Cup the three small petals by bending them inward.
2 • Place the three large petals just below the cupped petals.
3 • Twist all of the wires together and tape.

Tulip

Petals (continuous loops)
Make 1 (petal color) as follows:
1 • Leave 3" of bare wire.
2 • Make six 1" continuous loops.
3 • End with 3" of bare wire and cut from spool. Do not twist ends together.

Stamen
Make 1 (petal color) as follows:
1 • Cut 7" of bare wire.
2 • Place three beads in the center of the wire.
3 • Fold it in half and twist the entire length.

ASSEMBLY

1 • Center the stamen in the petals, making sure that the height of the stamen is equal to, or just below, the height of the petals.
2 • Twist the wire together and tape.

Detail of miniature iris and tulip.

Daffodil

Petals (continuous loops)

Make 1 (petal color) as follows:
1. Leave 3" of bare wire.
2. Make six ³⁄₄" continuous loops.
3. End with 3" of bare wire and cut from spool. Do not twist ends together.

Cup (continuous loops)

Make 1 (petal color) as follows:
1. Leave 3" of bare wire.
2. Make five ¹⁄₂" continuous loops.
3. End with 3" of bare wire and cut from spool. Do not twist ends together.

ASSEMBLY

1. Bend the cup petals up to form a circle.
2. Place circular cup piece in the center of the petal loops.
3. Twist all of the wires together and tape.

Leaves for Iris, Tulip, and Daffodil (loops)

Make 2 (green) per flower as follows:
1. Leave 1" of bare wire.
2. Using 4" of beads, make one loop.
3. End with 1" of bare wire and cut from spool.
4. Twist the wire and use floral tape to attach to flower stem.

Rose

Petals (continuous loops)

Make 1 (petal color) as follows:
1. Leave 3" of bare wire.
2. Using eight beads for each of the inner loops, make five two-row continuous loops.
3. End with 3" of bare wire and cut from spool. Do not twist ends together.

Make 1 (petal color) as follows:
1. Leave 3" of bare wire.
2. Using six beads for each of the inner loops, make four two-row continuous loops and one eight-bead single loop.
3. End with 3" of bare wire and cut from spool. Do not twist ends together.

Rose Leaves (continuous loops)

Make 1 (green) as follows:
1. Leave 1" of bare wire.
2. Using eight beads for each of the inner loops, make three two-row continuous loops.
3. End with 1" of bare wire, cut from the spool, and twist ends together.

ASSEMBLY

1. Using the petal group that has one small loop, arrange the petals so that the small loop is "standing up" in the center.
2. Place the petal group from step 1 in the center of the other and twist the wires together.
3. Tape the stem, positioning the leaf in an attractive position.

Detail of miniature daffodil and rose.

Swallowtail
Butterfly

Materials

- 4 strands color #1 (teal) 10/0 or 11/0 seed beads
- 2 strands color #2 (gold) 10/0 or 11/0 seed beads
- 1 strand color #3 (brown) 10/0 or 11/0 seed beads
- 26-gauge colored wire
- 18"-long 16-gauge stem wire
- ½" floral tape (brown or body color)
- Super glue
- **For jewelry items, add:**
  - E6000 glue
  - Pin finding
  - Black gloss paint (optional)
  - Super Glue

These are great as jewelry items or plant decorations. Because each one is made on a stem wire, you can then choose to leave "as is" or cut them loose.

swallowtail butterfly

Large wings (pointed top, round bottom)

Make 1: eight-bead basic, 15 rows.

1. Using bead color #1, complete rows 1 through 9.
2. Measure 24" of bare wire and cut the wing piece from the spool.
3. For rows 10 and 11, add 20 color #1 beads to the wire.
4. Add two beads of color #2 and two beads of color #3. Repeat that pattern six more times.
5. Add enough beads of color #1 to finish row 11.
6. For rows 12 and 13, begin with 20 color #1 beads.
7. Repeat step 4 and finish row 13 with color #1. As you work, compare rows 12 and 13 to the previous two to determine whether to add or subtract extra beads. The purpose is to get the two rows to "line up," creating two-row wing spots.
8. For row 14, begin with 20 color #1 beads and finish row with color #2.
9. On row 15, begin with enough color #2 beads to match the spotted area on row 13, add 10 beads of color #1, and then finish with color #3.
10. Leave three wires. Do not twist.

Make 1: eight-bead basic, 15 rows.

1. Using "reverse wrap" on all rows, make wing color patterns the same as the previously completed wing.
2. To reverse wrap, make the basic wire and loop as usual. However, each time you end a row, wrap the beaded wire under, and then over, the basics. You will be creating the wing from the backside, thereby producing a mirror image.

Small Wings
(pointed top, pointed bottom)

Make 2: eight-bead basic, nine rows.

1. Using color #1, complete rows 1 through 8.
2. Measure 6" of bare wire and cut the wing piece from the spool.
3. Add three color #2 beads, two color #3 beads, and three color #2 beads to the top basic wire.
4. To the cut wire, add on three color #2 beads, two color #3 beads, two color #2 beads, and one color #3 bead.

Bring the wire up the left side of the beads on the basic wire (right side if left-handed) and complete the row.
Note: If the colors don't line up, add or subtract beads as necessary.

5. Match the colors to produce stripes and bead back down the opposite side to the main portion of the wing.
6. Complete row 9 in color #1.
7. Leave three wires. Do not twist.
8. Decide whether your butterfly should have just legs, just antennae, or both legs and antennae. If you want both, cut a 6" piece of wire for the antennae and fold it in half. (This can also be two 6" pieces twisted together and then folded in half.)

(continued)

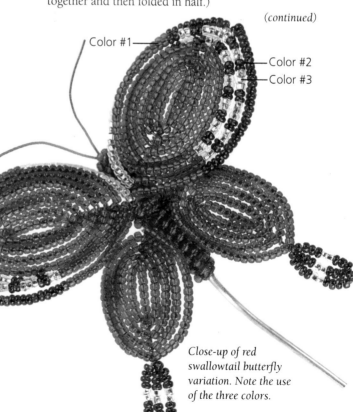

Color #1
Color #2
Color #3

Close-up of red swallowtail butterfly variation. Note the use of the three colors.

ASSEMBLY

1• Lightly tape the top 2" of the stem wire.

2• On all of the wings, spread the basic wires apart so they are easy to identify.

3• With "wrong" sides facing up, lay a small wing on top of a large wing.

4• Match the bases of the wings and twist only the center wires together.

5• Repeat with the other set.

6• Spread the wings open slightly.

7• Hold the two sections together with the wrong sides facing outward. (The prettiest sides are inside the "sandwich.") You are now displaying 10 wires; two are twisted, eight are not.

8• Choosing one untwisted wire from each side, twist them together, two at a time. You should now have six twisted wires (legs). Open the wings slightly.

Note: If you have chosen to have just legs, bend three of the wires to the right and three to the left.

If you have chosen to have just antennae, bend three of the wires sharply forward, and bend three wires sharply backward.

If you want both, space the legs as above. Thread the folded piece of wire behind the butterfly's front legs. Twist the ¹/₂" of wire closest to the legs and position

Try using a combination of three other bead colors for a completely new look to the same pattern.

the antennae forward. At this stage, it is OK if the antennae are floppy.

9• Using wire containing color #2 beads, begin wrapping 1" from the taped end of the stem wire. Use at least three wraps of bare wire to position the wire at the very tip of taped end. Tug on the wire to make sure it is secure.

10• Position the underside of the butterfly on the stem wire so that its center (point where all of the wings meet) is ⁵/₈" from the tip of the stem wire and the antennae are hanging off the end. If you are not making legs, three twisted wires should extend beyond the tip.

11• Slide the beads on the wire forward and begin beading the body. After four or five wraps (about ¹/₂"), pull the two front legs forward. Wrap once or twice and pull the second set of legs forward. Do the same to position the last set. When you arrive at the center point of the wings (probably between sets of legs) wrap one beaded wire over and between the wings. Pull the bead wrap very tight.

12• Continue wrapping until you have 1¹/₂" of body. Let the beads slide back and use three wraps tight against the beads to finish.

13• Bend and trim the legs and antennae. If you have no legs, trim off one of the three twisted wires at the tip.

14• Trim off any exposed floral tape or wires that extend beyond the tail.

15• On the tip and tail end of the body, very carefully place a very small drop of "super type" glue on the stem wire. Tilt the butterfly so that the glue runs under the first row of beads. Never put glue on the visible surface of the beads as it will dull the shine.

16• The butterfly is now ready to be used in a bouquet by bending the stem wire to the desired angle. To make a pin, refer to the bee instructions, page 85.

TIP: If there is glue visible after drying, use manicure scissors and tweezers to remove the excess. If the cut ends of the stem wire are noticeable, use a very fine brush to paint them black.

Tulip Poplar

*S*ince these blooms usually appear in the top branches of very tall trees, you don't get to see them very often. This one dropped, intact, and was "rescued" by my hubby. The unusual form "begged" to be beaded.

tulip poplar

Petals (round top, round bottom)

Make 6 (pale yellow and orange): eight-bead basic, 15 rows.

1 • Cut 3 feet of gold 26-gauge wire.
2 • Put eight orange beads on the wire and form the basic wire and loop.
3 • Begin the remaining rows with yellow beads. However, add six orange beads to rows 2 and 3, and eight orange beads to rows 4 and 5. Position the orange beads so that the bottom of the orange area is even with the bottom of the orange basic row. The top of the orange area will zigzag across the petal.
4 • Continue adding six orange to two rows, followed by eight orange to two rows, until completed.
5 • Reduce to two wires, cut from spool, and twist.

Stamens

Make 18 (yellow) as follows:

1 • Cut 18 6"-long pieces of 30-gauge gold wire.
2 • Put 2" of yellow beads on each wire.
3 • Hold the beads in place, 1" from one of the ends.
4 • Thread the long end of the wire back through all but the closest bead. (The bead closest to the long end.)
5 • When you have completed six, twist the bottom wires together so you end up with three groups of six.

Pistil (round top, round bottom)

Make 1 (green): ¹⁄₂" basic, nine rows.

1 • Leave three wires and twist.
2 • Twist the entire petal into a spiral.

Sepals (pointed top, round bottom)

Make 6 (green): ¹⁄₂" basic, 15 rows.

1 • Reduce to two wires and twist.
2 • Hold a pencil up the center front of each sepal and gently curl the sepals halfway around the pencil.

Leaf Sections

Make 4 (green): 1" basic, nine rows.

1 • Do not cut or fold the basic wires.
2 • Reduce to one wire.

Materials

• 1 hank pale yellow beads
• 3 strands orange beads
• 1½ hanks light green beads
• 26-gauge gold or yellow wire
• 26-gauge green wire (leaves, pistil, and sepals)
• 18"-long 16-gauge (or heavier) stem wire
• 30-gauge gold and green lacing and assembly wire
• ½" brown floral tape

FLOWER ASSEMBLY

1 • Lightly tape stem wire.

2 • Hold the base of the pistil even with the end of the stem wire and use assembly wire to secure it in place.

3 • Position the stamen groups around the pistil and wire them in place.

4 • Wire three petals directly below the stamens.

5 • Add the last three petals below and between the first three.

6 • One at a time, add the six sepals, with curved sides facing upward.

7 • Trim all of the wires to different lengths and use the end of the assembly wire to secure them against the stem.

Detail of tulip poplar, which combines two-colored petals, pale yellow stamens, and a green pistil for a stunning result.

LEAF ASSEMBLY

1• Stack two leaf sections together and twist the wires together lightly. Do the same to the other two sections.

2• Cut three 6" pieces of 30-gauge green wire.

3• Open one of the two leaf section groups so that the bottom, side edges are touching.

4• Beginning at the stem, use one piece of cut lacing wire to lace the sides together for $^{1}/_{2}$". Leave the lacing wire connected, as shown in Figure 53 below.

5• Open the other set of leaves and position them so that the bottom, side edges touch the previous group.

6• Twist the wires of the two groups together.

7• Using the green beads on green wire, begin at the base of the laced leaves and bead down until you meet the second group. Let the beads slide away and wrap bare wire twice around the bottom. Leave this beaded wire connected.

8• Use the last two pieces of cut lacing wire to lace the lower leaf sections to the ones they now touch. As

before, begin at the stem, lace $^{1}/_{2}$", and leave the wire connected.

9• Bring the beaded wire down to the new twisted stem.

10• Wrap it once around the base of the leaf group and then bead around the entire group as if it were a single petal. When you get to a basic wire, wrap around it. When you get to a valley, push the beads tightly into the crack and use a loop of the connected lacing wire to secure.

11• Continue in the same manner until you have gone completely around three times.

12• To end, wrap bare wire twice around the base and then spiral down the length of the twisted stem.

13• Trim and cover with floral tape.

14• Position the completed leaf about 2" below the flower and wire in place.

15• Tape all assembly areas with brown floral tape.

The leaf section of the tulip poplar begins with four 1"-basic, nine-row pieces that are then laced together, as shown in the illustrations at right.

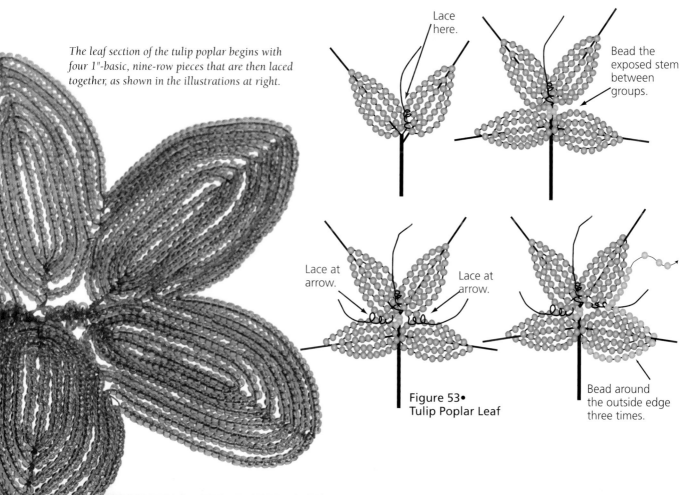

Lace here.

Bead the exposed stem between groups.

Lace at arrow.

Lace at arrow.

**Figure 53•
Tulip Poplar Leaf**

Bead around the outside edge three times.

Geranium

Materials

- 1½ hanks green 11/0 seed beads
- 1 hank pale yellow or white 11/0 seed beads
- ⅔-hank red, pink, salmon, or white 11/0 seed beads (increase to 1 hank for larger petals)
- 24- or 26-gauge colored beading wire
- 30-gauge gold wire
- 30-gauge green paddle wire (lacing and assembly)
- 5"-long 16-gauge stem wire
- 13"-long 16-gauge stem wire
- ½" green floral tape

Flowers (loops)

Make 18 (red) as follows:

1•Leave 6" of bare wire.

2•Using 1" of beads for the first loop, make five four-row crossover loops. (To make flowers with larger petals, you can make four three-row continuous loops.)

3•End with 6" of bare wire and cut from spool.

4•Bring one of the end wires up between the first two petals made and then back down between the last two petals made.

5•Put two yellow beads on the other wire end and bring the wire across the top of the flower. Center the yellow beads, pull the wire down on the other side of the flower, hold the two wires together, and twist.

Buds (crossover loops)

Make 10 (green) as follows:

1•Leave 6" of bare wire.

2•Using 1" of beads for the first loop, make one four-row crossover loop.

3•End with 6" bare wire, cut from the spool, twist the wire ends, and tape the 1" closest to the beads.

Make 4 (red and green) as follows:

1•Leave 6" of bare wire.

2•Using 1" of beads for the first loop, make one four-row crossover loop. Use red beads to make the first loop and green beads for the crossover.

3•End with 6" bare wire, cut from the spool, twist the ends, and tape the 1" closest to the beads.

Leaves (round top, round bottom)

Note: All nine of the leaves are made the same; however, each leaf is two rows larger than the previous one. After the green rows listed, each leaf has four rows of randomly mixed yellow and green beads, followed by two rows of solid yellow.

Make 1 (green and yellow): one-bead basic, 19 rows.

1•Begin by making your basic wire with two large basic loops. Do this by making the regular basic wire and loop with one full twist at the joint.

2•Form the second basic loop and wrap the wire once around the basic wire. Use pliers to flatten the twisted area as much as possible.

3•Use green beads for rows 1 through 13, but after row 3, cut one of the basic loops open at the bottom and pull the other loop out of the way.

4•Continue making rows at the bottom of the leaf by wrapping around the nearest cut wire and reverse directions. This will form the notch at the bottom, as shown (Figure 54).

5•After row 13, measure about 3 feet of bare wire and cut from spool.

6•Randomly mix green and yellow beads for rows 14 through 17.

7•Make rows 18 and 19 yellow.

8•When completed, bring the bare wire along the under side of the edge of the notch to the stem.

9•Wrap once around the stem, measure to the same length as the remaining basic loop, and cut.

(continued)

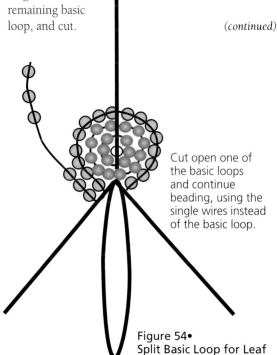

Cut open one of the basic loops and continue beading, using the single wires instead of the basic loop.

Figure 54•
Split Basic Loop for Leaf

10•Bend the cut basic wires along the top of the notch edge to the center.

11•Put enough green and yellow beads on each of these to match the edges of the notch.

12•Push the ends through the leaf and join them with the stem wires.

13•Twist all of the wires together and tape.

14•Trim and bend the top basic, as usual.

15•Lace the leaf.

16•Cut about 24" of 30-gauge gold wire.

17•In the center of the "V," attach the end of the wire to the outer row of beads.

18•Put seven yellow beads on the wire.

19•Skip six beads on the outer row and thread the wire around the outer row to secure.

20•Put seven more beads on the wire and proceed in the previous manner to apply scallops around the entire leaf.

Make 1 (green and yellow): one-bead basic, 21 rows.

Follow the same instructions as with the first leaf, except that rows 1 through 15 are green (step 3).

Make 1 (green and yellow): one-bead basic, 23 rows.

Follow the same instructions as with the first leaf, except that rows 1 through 17 are green (step 3).

Make 1 (green and yellow): one-bead basic, 25 rows.

Follow the same instructions as with the first leaf, except that rows 1 through 19 are green (step 3).

Make 1 (green and yellow): one-bead basic, 27 rows.

Follow the same instructions as with the first leaf, except that rows 1 through 21 are green (step 3).

Make 1 (green and yellow): one-bead basic, 29 rows.

Follow the same instructions as with the first leaf, except that rows 1 through 23 are green (step 3).

Make 1 (green and yellow): one-bead basic, 31 rows.

Follow the same instructions as with the first leaf, except that rows 1 through 25 are green (step 3).

Make 1 (green and yellow): one-bead basic, 33 rows.

Follow the same instructions as with the first leaf, except that rows 1 through 27 are green (step 3).

Make 1 (green and yellow): one-bead basic, 35 rows.

Follow the same instructions as with the first leaf, except that rows 1 through 29 are green (step 3).

ASSEMBLY

1• Lightly tape the stem wires.

2• Gather all of the bud pieces together, making sure that the tops are even and the red buds are in the center of the group. About ¾" from the buds, wrap assembly wire around the bundle, twist all of the wires together, and tape.

3• Gather flowers into groups of three and twist together 1" from the flowers.

4• Gather all of the groups together and position them so that they form a half-sphere.

5• Bring the wires together and twist. Use assembly wire to attach this grouping to the 5" stem wire.

6• Thin the twisted wires, if necessary, and tape the entire stem.

7• Beginning at the top of the stem wire, use assembly wire to attach the smallest leaf. Allow 2" to 3" of the leaf's stem to extend beyond the tip.

8• Wrap the assembly wire about ¾" down the stem and add the next largest leaf. Continue down the stem, adding all the leaves, the flowers, and the buds at attractive heights.

9• Tape the entire stem, starting at the base of the smallest leaf.

Create interest and realism with a subtle variation in bead colors, as in the geranium leaf shown here.

Although small in size, the geranium's bright red flowers make a giant impact.

Bird of Paradise

I love these flowers! As a matter of fact, I have one in my "new" backyard, as well as in my flower case. This pattern is slightly smaller than a live flower. If you decide to increase the petal size, to produce a larger flower, I suggest leaving the leaves the same size.

bird of paradise

Materials

- ¾-hank bright orange 11/0 seed beads
- 2 strands dark blue 11/0 seed beads
- 2 hanks medium green 11/0 seed beads
- 24- or 26-gauge beading wire
- 30-gauge painted floral paddle wire
- 4 18"-long 16-gauge stem wires
- ½" green floral tape

Petals (pointed top, round bottom)
Make 8 (orange): 2" basic, seven rows.
  Reduce each to one wire and lace.

"Stamens"
Make 3 (dark blue) as follows:
1. Cut 18" of 30-gauge paddle wire.
2. Place ¾" of beads on the wire.
3. Hold the beads 2" from one of the ends and thread the long wire back through all but the bead closest to the long end, as shown (Figure 55).
4. Place 2¾" of beads on the wire.
5. Skipping the bead closest to the end, thread the long wire back through ¾" of the beads.
6. Place 1" of beads on the wire.
7. Skipping the bead closest to the end, thread back through the beads.
8. Place ¾" of beads on the wire.
9. Skipping the bead closest to the end, thread back through the beads.
10. Place 2¾" of beads on the wire.
11. Skipping the bead closest to the end, thread back through ¾" of the beads.
12. Twist the bottom wires, and if the top beads appear loose, twist the top portion, just until firm.

Pods (pointed top, round bottom)
Make 2 (green): 2" basic, nine rows.
  Reduce each to one wire and lace.

Leaves (pointed top, round bottom)
Make 2 (green): 2" basic, 33 rows.
1. Use an 18" stem wire, placed against the back of the basic, to stiffen, as in Stem Stiffening Option 1, page 16.
2. Lace each leaf three times: at one-quarter, one-half, and three-quarters of its length.
3. Use floral tape to cover the exposed stem.

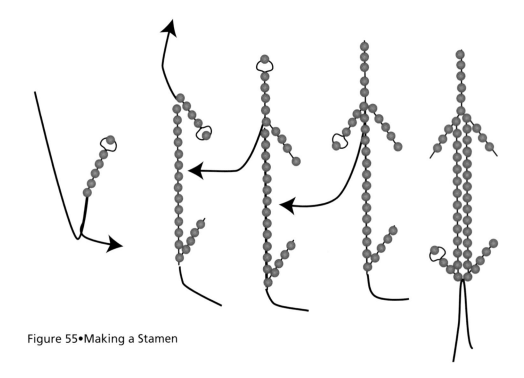

Figure 55•Making a Stamen

ASSEMBLY

1· Lightly tape the two remaining stem wires.

2· Bend all of the petals and pods into troughs.

3· Hold a stem wire and a pod together so that the tip of the stem wire extends 1½" above the base of the pod and is positioned inside the trough.

4· Secure with assembly wire.

5· Place one of the petals inside the pod, match the bases, and secure. Use a short piece of 30-gauge wire to thread through the center of the pod, through the petal, and then back down through the pod. Make sure to capture the stem wire. Twist and snip the ends.

6· Add one stamen and two more petals, making sure to match the bases.

7· Wrap the assembly wire down the stem to secure all of the untrimmed petal stems.

8· Cover the area with a light layer of tightly applied floral tape.

9· Bead 3" of the stem, starting at the base of the flower. Set aside.

10· Assemble the second flower in the same manner, using one pod, one petal, one stamen, two petals, one stamen, and the last two petals.

11· Bead 1" of stem, but do not cut the bead wire.

12· Hold the two blossoms together so they face in opposite directions and with the bottom of the beaded areas aligned.

13· Use assembly wire to tightly bind the stems together.

14· Continue wrapping beads down for another 8".

15· Match the beads on the leaf stems to the beads on the flower stem, bind the leaves in place with assembly wire, and bead down another 1".

16· Trim the bottom of the stem and cover with floral tape.

The bird of paradise flower comes together beautifully by assembling the bright-colored petals, stamens, and pods together and then finishing with a sturdy beaded stem.

Mexican Thistle

Materials

- 1 hank light green or metal-lined green 11/0 seed beads
- 1 hank light gray 11/0 seed beads
- 1 hank clear 11/0 seed beads
- 26-gauge green floral or beading wire
- 30-gauge floral wire (assembly)
- 2 18"-long 16-gauge stem wires
- ½" green floral tape

Centers (continuous loops)

Make 2 (green, gray, and clear) as follows:

1• String the wire with a random mix of beads, consisting of four strands of green, two strands of gray, and two strands of clear beads.

2• Leave 2" of bare wire.

3• Using 1½" of beads per loop and leaving about ⅛" bare wire between loops, make 48 continuous loops.

4• End with 2" of bare wire and cut from spool. Do not twist ends together.

Large Petals (pointed top, round bottom)

Make 18 (green, gray, and clear): 2" basic, five rows.

1• String the wire with a random mix of one part green, two parts gray, and two parts clear beads.

2• When row 5 is complete, bring the top basic wire forward and thread it, front to back, through the last two rows, on the left, as shown (Figure 56). Pull it straight up and trim to ⅛", creating a "thorn" on the petal tip.

3• Reduce to one wire and twist.

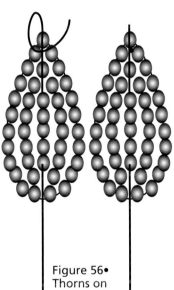

Figure 56•
Thorns on
Leaf Tips

Small Petals
(pointed top, round bottom)

Make 18 (green, gray, and clear): 1¾" basic, three rows.

1• String the wire with a random mix of one part green, two parts gray, and two parts clear beads.

2• When row 3 is complete, bring the top basic wire forward and thread it, front to back, through the last two rows, on the left. Pull it straight up and trim to ⅛", creating a "thorn" on the petal tip.

3• Reduce to one wire and twist.

I took a few liberties with this pattern. They call that artistic license, don't they? I love the little thorns on the leaf tips. To create the silvery green color of this desert wildflower, randomly mix your selected beads.

Mexican thistle

ASSEMBLY

1• Lightly tape the two stem wires.

2• Using one of the center pieces, position it so that the bottom of the first loop is even with the tip of a stem wire.

3• Wrap the bare wire tightly around the stem to secure.

4• Wrap the loops tightly down the stem, extending no more than 1" down.

5• Wrap the end bare wire down the stem to secure and fold all of the loops upward.

6• Using assembly wire, attach six large petals directly below the center piece.

7• Attach six small petals, directly below and between the large petals.

8• Feather the exposed wires to random lengths, secure, and cover with floral tape.

9• Repeat for the second flower.

10• Hold the two stems together and use assembly wire to bind the lower portions of the stems together approximately 5" from the flowers.

11• Where the two stems meet, attach six large petals, followed by six small petals.

12• Trim the wires, secure, and use floral tape to conceal any remaining assembly areas.

Close-up of Mexican thistle.

Texas
Bluebonnet

Materials

- 1 hank medium or dark blue 11/0 seed beads
- 1 strand white 11/0 seed beads
- 1 strand red 11/0 seed beads
- ½-hank medium green 11/0 seed beads
- 24- or 26-gauge colored beading wire
- 30-gauge assembly wire
- 18"-long 16-gauge stem wire
- ½" green floral tape

This western lupine incorporates several unusual uses of shape and color. However, it wasn't until I was done making this flower that I discovered why they were called bluebonnets. Oops! Pinch, shape, pinch, shape—got it!

Texas bluebonnet

Top Petals (flat top, pointed bottom)

Make 8 (blue and red): one-bead basic, nine rows.

1. Cut 20" of beading wire and form a basic wire and basic loop.
2. Use a red bead for the basic.
3. For rows 2 and 3, use eight beads each and begin and end each row with two red beads.
4. Begin row 4 and end row 5 with two red beads.
5. Begin row 6 and end row 7 with one red bead.
6. Make rows 8 and 9 solid blue.
7. After finishing row 9, support the petal while using pliers to pull the top basic wire sharply back and downwards. This will cause a dip in the top of the petal, creating a heart shape. Trim and hide the basic.
8. Reduce to one wire and twist.

Make 8 (blue and white): one-bead basic, nine rows.

1. Cut 20" of beading wire and form basic wire and basic loop.
2. Use a white bead for the basic row.
3. For rows 2 and 3, use eight beads each and begin and end each row with two white beads.
4. Begin row 4 and end row 5 with two white beads.
5. Begin row 6 and end row 7 with one white bead.
6. Make rows 8 and 9 solid blue.
7. After finishing row 9, support the petal while using pliers to pull the top basic wire sharply back and downwards. This will cause a dip in the top of the petal, creating a heart shape. Trim and hide the basic.
8. Reduce to one wire and twist.

Make 4 (blue, white, and red): one-bead basic, nine rows.

1. Cut 20" of beading wire and form a basic wire and basic loop.
2. Use a red bead for the basic row.
3. For rows 2 and 3, use eight beads each and begin and end each row with two red beads.
4. Begin row 4 and end row 5 with two white beads.
5. Begin row 6 and end row 7 with one white bead.
6. Make rows 8 and 9 solid blue.
7. After finishing row 9, support the petal while using pliers to pull the top basic wire sharply back and downwards. This will cause a dip in the top of the petal, creating a heart shape.
8. Reduce to one wire and twist.

Lower Petals (loops)

Make 24 (blue) as follows:

1. Leave 2" of bare wire.
2. Using ½" of beads for the first row, make a double-row continuous loop with a one-row crossover.
3. End with 2" of bare wire, cut from spool, and twist ends together.

Large Buds (continuous loops)

Make 8 (blue) as follows:

1. Leave 2" of bare wire.
2. Using ½" of beads for the first row, make a triple-row continuous loop.
3. End with 2" of bare wire and cut from spool.
4. Hold the pieces together in pairs and twist (four total pairs).

Medium Buds (continuous loops)

Make 4 (green) as follows:

1. Leave 2" of bare wire.
2. Using ½" of beads for the first row, make a double-row continuous loop with a one-row crossover.
3. End with 2" of bare wire, cut from spool, and twist ends together.

Small Buds (crossover continuous loops)

Make 8 (green) as follows:

1. Leave 2" of bare wire.
2. Using ½" of beads for the first row, make one crossover continuous loop.
3. End with 2" of bare wire, cut from spool, and twist ends together.

Leaves (pointed top, round bottom)

Make 2 (green): 1" basic, seven rows.
Reduce each to one wire and twist.

Make 2 (green): 1¼" basic, nine rows.
Reduce each to one wire and twist.

Make 1 (green): 1½" basic, 11 rows.
Reduce to one wire and twist.

(continued)

ASSEMBLY

1• Lightly tape the stem wire and set aside.

2• Matching the lower beads, twist a lower petal together with each of the upper petals. (The four remaining lower petals will be used as medium blue buds.)

3• Turn the lower petal so that it is perpendicular to the upper petal.

4• Use floral tape, cut in half lengthwise, to tape the top 1" of each of the flower stems and the top ¹/₂" of each of the bud stems.

5• Using assembly wire, start at the top and begin attaching buds and flowers in the following pattern, which is also shown in Figure 57:

  a• Place one small bud at the tip and cluster the remaining seven small green buds directly below.

  b• Drop down ¹/₄" and add four medium green buds.

  c• Drop down ¹/₂" and add four medium blue buds.

  d• Drop down 1" and add four large blue buds.

  e• Drop down 1" and add four blue and white flowers.

  f• Drop down 1" and add four blue and white flowers.

  g• Drop down 1" and add four blue, red and white flowers.

  h• Drop down 1" and add four blue and red flowers.

  i• Drop down 1" and add four blue and red flowers.

6• Gather all of the leaves together, match the bases, and twist the wires.

7• Fan them open into a small-medium-large-medium-small pattern.

8• Use floral tape to cover the top 1¹/₂" of the stem.

9• Secure the leaf group about 4" below the lowest flower.

10• Use floral tape to cover all assembly areas.

Detail of Texas bluebonnet.

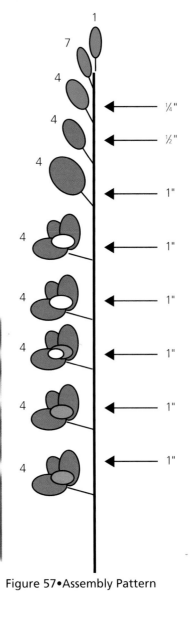

Figure 57•Assembly Pattern

Simple
Bonsai Tree

I get a lot of requests for bonsai trees. So, I "finally" gave in and produced one that won't take you six months to finish. A hank of beads and a paddle of wire are all that is needed for this delightful little tree.

simple bonsai tree

Materials

- 1 hank green 11/0 seed beads
- ¼ lb. paddle 26-gauge black or green floral wire

TIP: While making branches, <u>always</u> make all of the twists in the same direction. The easiest way to approach this tree is to make three small branches, then use them to make one medium branch. When you have completed three medium branches, make one large branch. When you have four large branches, make a tree.

Leaves
Make 108 (green) as follows:
1• Cut a 36" piece of wire.
2• Place 2" of beads in the center and fold in half.
3• Twist the beads until you form a loose ball.
4• Twist 1" of the wire directly below the beads.
5• Set aside and make two more (Figure 58).

Small Branch
Make 36 (green) as follows:
1• Hold three leaf pieces with the tips fairly even.
2• Twist together for 1" below the previously twisted area, as shown (Figure 59).

Medium Branch
Make 12 (green) as follows:
1• Using three small branches, hold two of them together, slightly offset, and twist 1" of the untwisted wire.
2• Place the third small branch below the twisted area, as shown (Figure 60), and twist for 1".

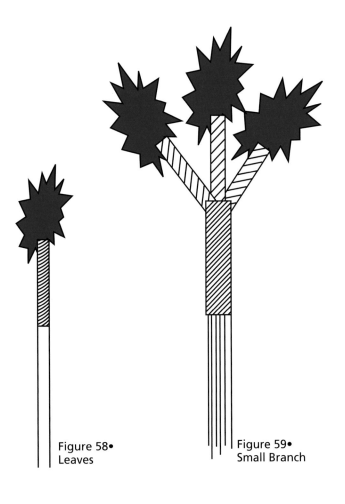

Figure 58•
Leaves

Figure 59•
Small Branch

Figure 60•
Medium Branch

Large Branch

Make 4 (green) as follows:

1•Using three medium branches, hold two of them together, slightly offset, and twist 1" of the untwisted wire.

2•Place the third medium branch below the twisted area and twist again for 1" (Figure 61).

Tree

1•Select a branch to be the tree's top.

2•Position the other three large branches down the trunk and slightly below each other.

3•Tightly twist all but the bottom 5" of the trunk (Figure 62).

Roots

1•Divide the bottom wires into five slightly uneven groups.

2•Twist each of them in the opposite direction of the trunk, until they have a gnarled appearance.

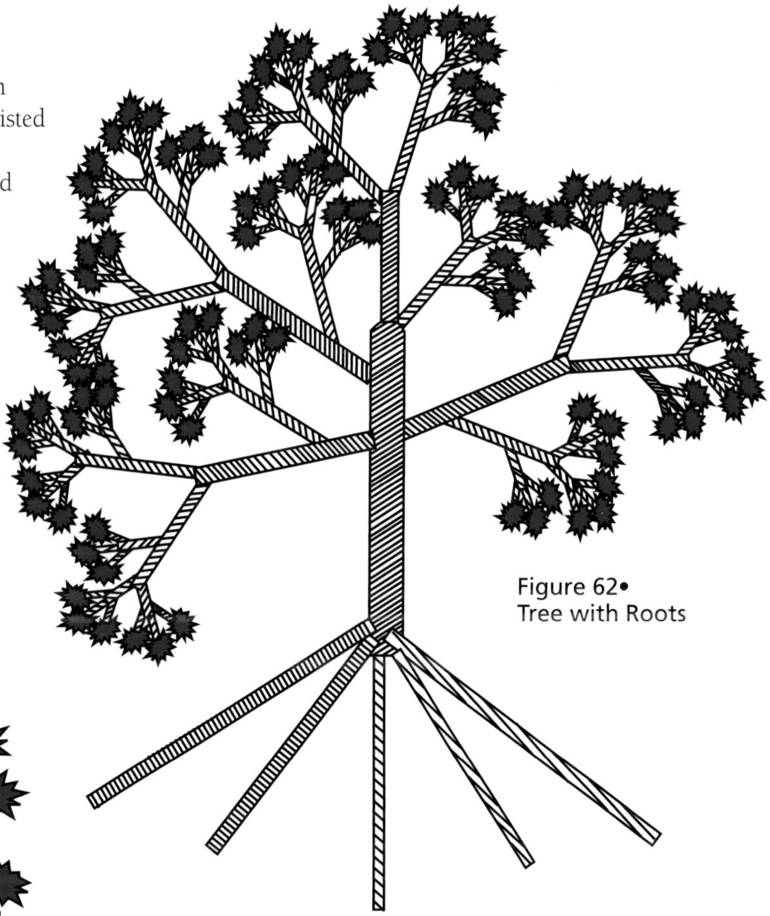

Figure 62•
Tree with Roots

Detail of bonsai branch ends, which are readily accomplished with with some twisting.

Figure 61•
Large Branch

Large
Sunflower

Materials

- 3 hanks yellow 11/0 beads
- 3 hanks green 11/0 beads
- 1 hank brown 11/0 beads
- 26-gauge beading wire
- 24-gauge green floral paddle or beading wire
- 30-gauge gold and green lacing wire
- 3 12"-long pieces of 22-gauge wire (to stiffen leaf stems)
- 24" ¼"-diameter copper tubing
- 2½"-diameter circle of brown Foamie craft foam
  or light cardboard
- Green floral tape
- E 6000 or hot glue (optional)

This cheery flower measures more than 8" across the center. If you want an exceptionally stable flower, I have included an optional step that is guaranteed to hold this large, heavy flower together. I have to admit that I would not recommend it for arrangements—unless, of course, you are making an arrangement the size of a Volkswagen Beetle.

large sunflower

Petals (pointed top, round bottom)

Make 18 (yellow): 1¼" basic, 13 rows.
1. After completing each petal, leave two wires and twist only ¼" of the stem closest to the petal.
2. Lace each petal across the center.

Make 18 (yellow): 1½" basic, 13 rows.
1. After completing each petal, leave two wires and twist only ¼" of the stem closest to the petal.
2. Lace each petal across the center.

Sepals (pointed top, round bottom)

Make 9 (green): ½" basic, 11 rows.
Leave three wires and twist.

Center (round)

Make 1 (brown): one-bead basic, 30 rows.
1. Before beginning, make sure that your top basic wire is at least 5" long and your basic loop is large enough to fit loosely around your hand.
2. Since you will end at the top of the circle, cut the wire and twist it with the top basic wire.
3. Twist the bottom loop.
4. Lace the center three times: once across the center and twice to form an "X" across the back.

Leaves (pointed top, round bottom)

Make 3 (green): ½" basic, 41 rows.
1. After completing each leaf, leave three wires and twist.
2. To strengthen the stems, use 12" of 22-gauge wire and Stem Stiffening Option 2, page 16.
3. Lace each leaf three times: once across the center and twice to form an "X".
4. Use beaded wire to wrap 2" of the stem, closest to the petal.

ASSEMBLY

1. Use one large petal and one small to make 18 pairs. Twist them together for ½" below the petals.

2. About ¼" from the edge of your foam (or cardboard) circle, poke 18 evenly spaced small holes.

3. Slip a pair of petals into each of these holes. Arrange them so that they are evenly spaced around the edge of the circle and lay this face down on a flat surface.

4. On the back of the circle, separate one wire from each pair of petals. Twist it firmly with one wire from the pair immediately next to it. Trim the twisted wires to ½" and fold them firmly toward the center.

5. Position the brown center over the front of the circle and thread the wires between the petals, directly across from each other. Bring them to the center back, twist the ends together, and fold them flat against the circle.

6. Twist the remaining wires lightly. Test the fit to make sure that they will slip inside the copper tubing. If they will not fit, taper and trim the wires until you are able to push the tubing all the way to the back of the flower.

(continued)

7• Place a generous amount of glue inside the tubing and insert the flower. If you are using hot glue, you must work quickly. If the glue hardens too quickly, carefully heat the tubing to soften the glue.

8• Optional* but recommended: For added stability, you may leave the circle in place and fill the back of the circle with hot glue or E6000®. If you do this, pull the edges of the circle toward the back, between the petals, and secure them in the glue. This will make the circle smaller and keep it out of sight.

*If you are happy with the stability of the petals and choose not to add the additional glue, simply cut and remove the circle.

9• Once the glue hardens, use floral tape to cover the entire stem.

10• Use assembly wire to attach the sepals, three at a time, directly below the flower. Position them with the wrong side toward the flower and the sepals curved upward.

Regardless of how you have the large sunflower positioned as it adorns a deck or table, you can be sure it will impress. The front is gorgeous with its swirling center, beaded stem, and tremendous petals and leaves.

11• Position the leaves at attractive levels and securely wrap them in place with 26-gauge wire.

12• Cover the assembly areas with floral tape.

13• Cover the entire stem with beaded wire. Begin at the top in the area between the sepals and the flower.

14• End approximately 4" from the bottom by wrapping several times around the tubing with bare wire. Continue wrapping the bare wire to the bottom and cover it with floral tape.

15• Arrange the petals so that all of the short petals are pulled to the front and the flower appears to have three to four layers of petals.

16• "Plant" in a well-weighted pot.

The back does not disappoint either with its view of the beaded stem and sepals that strategically hide the center work area.

Christmas Cactus

f you have already made other flowers, be prepared. In order to solve the assembly problems, I created this one a little upside-down. Make this beauty in pink, red, white or salmon for your holiday cheer.

Christmas cactus

Materials

- 1 hank petal-colored 11/0 seed beads
- 1 hank green 11/0 seed beads
- 18 3mm yellow beads
- 4 20-gauge stem wires
- 24- or 26-gauge green wire
- 24- or 26-gauge petal-colored beading wire
- Krazy Glue (optional)
- ½" floral tape

Detail of Christmas cactus flower, a festive addition to your holiday home-decorating stash.

Petals (15 per flower; pointed top, round bottom)

Make 54 (petal color): 10 bead basic, five rows.
Reduce each to one wire.

Leaves (round top, round bottom)

Make 2 "three-segment" (green) as follows:
1•Begin with a 2½" basic row on a 12" top basic wire.
2•Hold one of the 20-gauge stem wires against the back and incorporate it into the construction.
3•Complete eight rows.
4•At the top, wrap the bare wire up the basic for ¼".
5•Add 2" of beads to the top basic wire.
6•Use this to form the next leaf segment.
7•Complete six rows.
8•At the top, wrap the bare wire up the basic for ¼".
9•Add 1½" of beads to the top basic wire.
10•Use this to form the next leaf segment.
11•Complete six rows.
12•Wrap the wire once around the top.
13•Leaving the 20-gauge wire alone, measure 12" of bare beading wire and cut.
14•Lace all segments.

Make 2 "two-segment" (green) as follows:
1•Begin with a 2" basic row on a 10" top basic wire.
2•Hold one of the 20-gauge stem wires against the back and incorporate it into the construction.
3•Complete six rows.
4•At the top, wrap the bare wire up the basic for ¼".
5•Add 1½ " of beads to the top basic wire.
6•Use this to form the next leaf segment.
7•Complete six rows.
8•Wrap the wire once around the top.
9•Leave 2" of the 20-gauge wire and cut.
10•Measure 12" of the bare beading wire and cut.
11•Lace all segments.

Make 2 (green): 2½" basic, eight rows.
1•Use the 20-gauge wire that was cut from the two-segment leaf to stiffen.
2•End at the top.
3•Leave 12" of beading wire and cut.

ASSEMBLY

1· Choose the three leaves that will have buds and set them aside.

2· With the "right" sides out, hold three petals (one in front, two in back) so that the beaded bases are even with the top of a segmented leaf. The petal wires should be pointed up along the bare 20-gauge wire (upside-down), as shown (Figure 63).

3· Wrap the 12" beading wire once around them to secure.

4· Twist the three petal wires together.

5· Add three more petals (two in front, one in back) in the same manner.

6· Continue to add alternating batches of petals until you have 15 petals.

7· Tightly wrap the wire two or three more times.

8· Leaving the 20-gauge wire, cut all other wires as close as possible to the wrapped area.

9· Place a drop of glue on the wrapped wire. Do not get any on the beads.

10· Slide six 3mm yellow beads on the 20-gauge wire and push them tightly against the wrapped area.

11· Fold the 20-gauge wire down tightly against the beads. Leave no more than $1/8$" of bent wire and cut it off. This bent tip should hold the 3mm beads in place.

12· Pull the petals toward the tip then curl them back up.

13· Repeat with two more of the segmented leaves. Set aside.

14· On the three remaining leaves, you will be making buds. Choose either green or petal-colored beads.

15· For small buds, string $1\frac{1}{2}$" of beads on the 12" wire.

16· Make a $3/4$" crossover loop on the tip, wrap the wire an extra time or two around the base of the bud, and cut. Place a drop of glue on the wrapped area.

17· For large buds, use 2" of petal-colored beads and complete as in step 16.

18· Gather all of the leaf stems together, wrap with wire, trim, and tape.

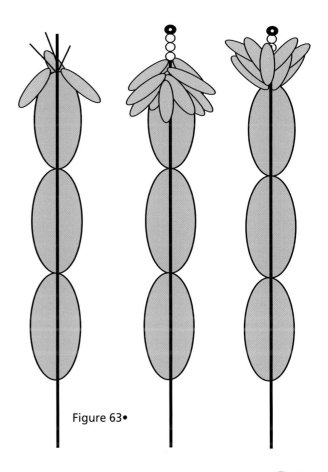

Figure 63•

TIP: For a larger plant, simply make multiples of this pattern. If you want a wider plant, add several four-segment leaves. The first segment would then have a 3" basic with eight rows. Complete the rest of the leaf as you would the three-segment size.

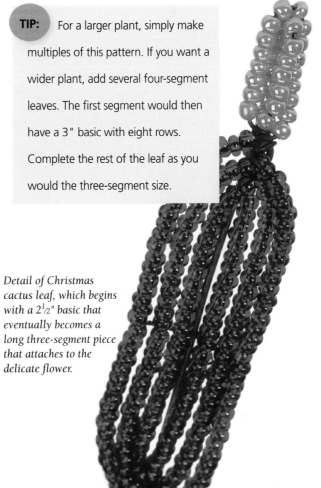

Detail of Christmas cactus leaf, which begins with a $2\frac{1}{2}$" basic that eventually becomes a long three-segment piece that attaches to the delicate flower.

Poinsettia with Pinecone and Branch

Materials

- **For poinsettia:**
  - 1 hank red, pink, or cream-colored beads
  - ½-hank light or medium green beads
  - 54 yellow beads
  - 26-gauge red (or petal-colored) wire
  - 26-gauge green wire
  - 30-gauge assembly wire
  - 12" piece 22-gauge wire (cut in half and use to stiffen leaves)
  - 18" piece 16-gauge, or heavier, stem wire
  - ½" green floral tape
- **For pinecone and branch:**
  - 1 hank medium green 11/0 seed beads
  - ½-hank brown 11/0 seed beads
  - 1 strand white 11/0 seed beads (optional)
  - 24- or 26-gauge brown or black wire
  - 30-gauge green wire (needles and assembly)
  - 12" piece 16-gauge stem wire
  - Brown floral tape

You can use this flower in all of your holiday applications. It is guaranteed to keep its petals throughout the entire season. Actually, the petals are not petals at all. The poinsettia's flowers are the tiny nubbins in the center. The colored leaves at the top are really, just that, colored leaves, called bracts.

poinsettia with pinecone

Flowers (continuous crossover loops)

Make 1 (green, red, and yellow) as follows:

1 • Cut 30" of wire.
2 • String two green beads, two red beads, four yellow beads, two red beads, and then two more green beads.
3 • Push the beads into position 2" from one of the ends and make a loop.
4 • On the long end of the wire, add three green, two red, five yellow, two red, and three more green beads. Make the crossover loop.
5 • Repeat this process until you have six flowers.
6 • Bring the ends together and twist.

Bracts (pointed top, round bottom)

Make 5 (red, pink, or white): 1½" basic, nine rows.

Note: To maintain a sharp pointed tip, add a bead to the basic wire each time around.

1 • Make rows 1 through 5 as usual.
2 • After completing row 5, bring the beaded wire to within 1" of the top right side, fold it back down, and wrap it around the basic loop, as shown (Figure 64).
3 • Repeat this procedure on the other side. You now have nine rows across.
4 • Leave three wires and twist smoothly.
5 • Lace so that the lacing crosses no more than ½" below the tips of the outside rows.

Make 5 (red, pink, or white): 2" basic, 13 rows.

Note: To maintain a sharp pointed tip, add a bead to the basic wire each time around.

1 • Make rows 1 through 9 as usual.
2 • After completing row 9, bring the beaded wire to within 1" of the top right side, fold it back down, and wrap it around the basic loop.
3 • Repeat this procedure on the other side. You now have 13 rows across.

4 • Leave three wires and twist smoothly.
5 • Lace so that lacing crosses no more than ½" below the tips of the outside rows.

Leaves (pointed top, round bottom)

Make 2 (green): 2½" basic, 19 rows.

Note: To maintain a sharp pointed tip, add a bead to the basic wire each time around.

1 • Complete rows 1 through 11 as usual.
2 • After completing row 11, bring the beaded wire up to within 1¼" of the top right side, fold it back down, and wrap it around the basic loop.
3 • Repeat on the other side. You now have 15 rows across.

(continued)

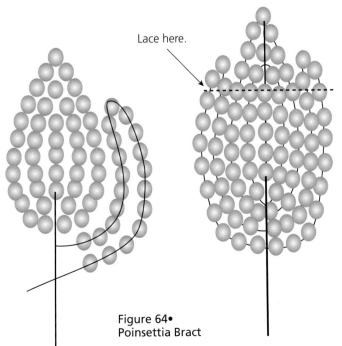

Lace here.

**Figure 64•
Poinsettia Bract**

4•Bring the beaded wire to within 1¼" of the previously folded wire on the right side.

5•Fold it back down and wrap.

6•Repeat on the left side. You now have 19 rows across.

7•Leave three wires and stiffen with Stem Stiffening Option 2, page 16.

8•Cut, twist, and tape the stems.

9•Lace each leaf twice, so that lacing crosses no more than ½" below the tips of the outside rows.

Cone "Petals" (round top, round bottom)

Note: If you would like "snowy tips," on the pinecone, end each even-numbered row and begin each odd-numbered row with three or four white beads.

Make 3 (brown): six-bead basic, three rows.

Make 15 (brown): six-bead basic, five rows.

Make 11 (brown): six-bead basic, seven rows.

Needles

Make 108 (green) as follows:

1•String the entire hank of green beads on the 30-gauge wire.

2•Leaving 3" of bare wire, skip the bead closest to the end, and thread the bare wire back through 2" of beads.

3•End with 1" of bare wire and cut from spool.

4•Each time you complete three needles, twist their wires together. You should end up with 36 three-needle groups.

Close-up of poinsettia: What a glorious centerpiece for your holiday table!

ASSEMBLY

For the poinsettia:

1· Lightly tape the stem wire.

2· Using assembly wire, attach the flower group to the tip on the stem.

3· Directly below the flowers, add the five small bracts. Leave at least 1/4" of the bare, twisted colored wire showing. Experiment with this measurement to determine the desired effect.

4· Add the five large bracts directly below, and between the small bracts.

5· Trim the remaining wires to different lengths.

6· Wrap the assembly wire approximately 2 1/2" down the stem and secure a leaf. Once again, leave a portion of the taped leaf stem showing.

7· Repeat for the second leaf.

8· Use floral tape to tape over all exposed assembly areas.

9· Optional: Mount together with pinecone and branch as I did in the sample shown.

For the pinecone and branch:

1· Gently give each pinecone "petal" a side-to-side "cup" shape.

2· Hold the three smallest petals together so that the tips are even.

3· Twist 1/2" of the wires, closest to the beads, together.

4· Position four medium petals so that the tips are about halfway down the length of the previous row.

5· Again, bring all of the wires together and twist about 1/2".

6· In the same manner, add five medium, six medium, five large, and then the last six large petals.

7· When completed, twist all of the remaining wires and tape with brown floral tape.

8· Lightly tape the stem wire.

9· Hold three needle groups with the base of the beads even with the end of the stem wire.

10· Secure with assembly wire.

11· Wrap the wire down the stem 1/2" and add three more needle groups.

12· Continue in the same manner until you reach the seventh row.

13· Attach the pinecone stem, along with three more needle groups.

14· Continue to attach the needle groups, three groups at a time, until complete.

15· Tape the entire stem.

Detail of pinecone.

Materials

- 4 strands green 11/0 seed beads
- 24- or 26-gauge green beading or paddle wire
- 30-gauge lacing wire
- 2" x 4" piece green Foamie or other stuffing material (optional)
- Gold paint (optional)
- Red ribbon (optional)

Pickle (slightly pointed top, slightly pointed bottom)

Make 3 (green): 2" basic, 11 rows.

1• Do not cut the top basic wires.

2• Leave three wires and twist lightly.

3• Leaving a 1" tail at the beginning and end, lace each piece three times: once in the center and once ½" from the top and bottom.

According to an old German tradition, the last decoration hidden on the Christmas tree was to be a pickle. The observant person who found it on Christmas Day was, supposedly, blessed with a year of good fortune and, of course, a special gift.

pickle ornament

ASSEMBLY

1• Lay all of the pieces wrong-side up on a flat surface, with their tips touching.

2• Tightly twist the top basic wires together.

3• Fold the pieces upward and twist the lacing wires together.

4• Placing your finger inside the tube, flatten the bottom and form it into a rounded cylinder.

5• Tightly roll the Foamie®, or other stuffing material, and slip it into the cylinder.

6• Close the top of the pickle by twisting all of the stem wires together.

7• Shape the stem wires into a hook and trim.

8• Dip the hook into gold paint and hang upside-down until completely dry.

9• Adorn with a small red bow.

Close-up of the Christmas pickle, which is a nice project for parents and children to make together and then use each year for a memorable family tradition.

Resources

There are many local bead specialty stores, as well as general crafting stores, that sell the supplies needed for French beading. Check your local listings for a store in your area, or visit one of the Web sites listed below.

Beaded Flower Patterns (my Web site)
www.beadedflowerpatterns.com
Krause Publications
French-Beaded Flowers: New Millennium Collection (my first book)
www.krause.com
Beading Retailers
http://members.cox.net/sdsantan/storelinks.html
General Craft Retailers
www.acmoore.com
www.artsandcraftscanada.com
www.craftcanada.com
www.hobbylobby.com
www.joanns.com
www.michaels.com

About the Author

Dalene Kelly runs her French-beaded flower business (Web site listed on preceding page) from her new surroundings in Yuma, Arizona.

First introduced to French beading in the late-1960s by her mother-in-law, Sally Kelly, Dalene did not pursue the art until the mid-1980s. In 1997, she retired from a 20-year career in retail management to pursue her passion for designing French-beaded flower patterns instead.

Since then, Dalene has taught many classes on the subject and authored *French-Beaded Flowers: New Millennium Collection* (Krause Publications, 2001). *Bead & Button Magazine* also featured her Phalaenopsis Orchid pattern on the cover of its October 2001 issue and that same year, Dalene served as co-designer and project coordinator for the Swarovski Crystal® Beaded Flower Collection.

When she is not French beading, she enjoys time with her loving husband, Van. They have four grown sons (Chad, Van Jr., Steven, and Christopher), a black Labrador retriever, and a conure. She further enjoys gardening, bird watching, reading, and traveling.

With Beads, The Possibilities Are Endless

French-Beaded Flowers
New Millennium Collection
by Dalene Kelly

Author Dalene Kelly will guide you with step-by-step instructions to make 38 different flowers, such as tiger lilies, trilliums, pansies, irises and gladiolas. You will then learn how to incorporate these unique flowers into four creative projects: a cymbidium corsage, rose hair barrette, Shasta daisy napkin ring and rose bud bridal veil.

Softcover • 8¼ x 10⅞
96 pages
55 color photos & 60 illus.
Item# FREBD • $18.95

Decorative Wirework
by Jane Davis

You'll find fresh, new and exciting ideas for working with wire in this new book from author Jane Davis. Create more than 50 projects, including earrings, brooches, bracelets, window treatments and candleholders with her easy-to-follow instructions, detailed illustrations and beautiful photographs. Projects are appropriate for all skill levels.

Softcover • 8¼ x 10⅞
128 pages
150+ color photos & 200 illus.
Item# DCWK • $19.95

The Complete Guide to Beading Techniques
30 Decorative Projects
by Jane Davis

This is the most complete volume of beading techniques on the market, filled with gorgeous photos of antique and contemporary beadwork that will inspire beaders of any skill level. After learning about the basic terms and tools, you will explore each technique, including beadweaving, crochet, and tambourwork, and complete a sampler to reinforce the skill learned. Finally, 30 elegant projects, such as table settings, Christmas ornaments, lampshades, a purse and a pincushion, ranging in difficulty from beginner to expert, are included.

Softcover • 8¼ x 10⅞ • 160 pages
175 charts & illus. • 150 color photos
Item# BEHME • $24.95

A Beader's Reference
by Jane Davis

Feel inspired to create beautiful beaded masterpieces with this reference offering a multitude of patterns for motifs and centerpieces, borders and cords, and fringes and edgings. The hundreds of easy-to-follow beading graphs and how-to illustrations can be your secret to looking like an accomplished beading professional. With three pattern sections, a project section with instructions for 12 projects and a contributing artists' gallery, this book provides more inspiration for creating beautiful beaded pieces than any other of its kind.

Softcover • 8¼ x 10⅞ • 160 pages
250+ charts & illus. • 130 color photos
Item# BDREF • $24.99

Quick & Easy Beaded Jewelry
by Elizabeth Gourley and Ellen Talbott

You'll find hours of fun and inspiration for making your own unique and fashionable beaded jewelry in this new book! Includes 30 lovely projects for making matching necklaces, bracelets, earrings, and rings using beading techniques such as stranding, peyote stitching, and netting. Detailed directions, lavish photography, and illustrations guide you through each project quickly and easily.

Softcover • 8¼ x 10⅞ • 128 pages
175+ illus. • 85 color photos
Item# QEBJ • $19.95

Beaded Jewelry with Found Objects
by Carole J. Rodgers

Match designer jewelry--reflective of your impeccable taste--with each outfit you own! With the more than 30 original projects using items that can be found in hardware stores, fishing tackle shops, flea markets, glass items, game pieces, cabochons, and other natural objects, and the inspiration to create more, you'll be beading gifts as individual as yourself. Projects, such as the Amethyst Crystal Necklace, which is made with a pie-shaped slice of amethyst crystal on a chain of amethyst and lavender seed beads, are photographed and accompanied by clear instructions.

Softcover • 8¼ x 10⅞ • 128 pages
225+ illus. • 150+ color photos
Item# BJFO • $19.99

TO ORDER, CALL (800) 258-0929 OFFER CRB4

kp

Krause Publications, Offer CRB4
P.O. Box 5009, Iola WI 54945-5009
www.krausebooks.com

Please add $4.00 for the first book and $2.25 each additional for shipping and handling to U.S. addresses. Non-U.S. addresses please add $20.95 for the first book and $5.95 each additional. Residents of CA, IA, IL, KS, NJ, PA, SD, TN, and WI, please add appropriate sales tax.